Jason Kelly created The Neatest Little Guide series to make complex information enjoyable. This is the fourth book in the series, preceded by *Mutual Fund Investing*, *Stock Market Investing*, and *Personal Finance*. Jason teaches financial seminars throughout California, participates in radio and television interviews, and publishes *The NeatSheet*, a monthly investment newsletter. You can reach him through his website at **www.jasonkelly.com**. He lives in Los Angeles.

**Also by Jason Kelly**

NONFICTION

*The Neatest Little Guide to Mutual Fund Investing*
*The Neatest Little Guide to Stock Market Investing*
*The Neatest Little Guide to Personal Finance*

FICTION

*Y2K—It's Already Too Late*

# The Neatest Little Guide to Making Money Online

JASON KELLY

A PLUME BOOK

PLUME
Published by the Penguin Group
Penguin Putnam Inc., 375 Hudson Street,
New York, New York 10014, U.S.A.
Penguin Books Ltd, 27 Wrights Lane,
London W8 5TZ, England
Penguin Books Australia Ltd, Ringwood,
Victoria, Australia
Penguin Books Canada Ltd, 10 Alcorn Avenue,
Toronto, Ontario, Canada M4V 3B2
Penguin Books (N.Z.) Ltd, 182–190 Wairau Road,
Auckland 10, New Zealand

Penguin Books Ltd, Registered Offices:
Harmondsworth, Middlesex, England

First published by Plume,
a member of Penguin Putnam Inc.

First Printing, January, 2000
3 5 7 9 10 8 6 4 2



LIBRARY OF CONGRESS CATALOGING-IN-PUBLICATION DATA:
Kelly, Jason.
The neatest little guide to making money online / Jason Kelly.
p. cm.
ISBN 0-452-28168-7
1. Electronic commerce. 2. Business enterprises—Computer networks.
3. Internet marketing. 4. World Wide Web (Information retrieval system)
I. Title.

HF5548.32.K45 2000
658.8'0025'4678—dc21
99-045730

Printed in the United States of America
Set in Times New Roman

# Ten Steps to Making Money Online

# Acknowledgments

This is the first Neatest Little Guide that doesn't cover money management. Instead, it covers a new way to make additional money so that you actually have something left to manage after the bills have been paid.

It took several discussions with the people closest to this series for me to embrace a new direction. Jennifer Kasius, my editor, has an eagle eye for sloppy writing and has developed a second sense for what a Neatest Little Guide should be. It's hard to imagine writing these books without her. We've worked on them together for so long that the series saw her last name change from Dickerson to Kasius after her wedding. Publishing years—like dog years—are much shorter than real years. By publishing standards, Jennifer and I have worked together on the Neatest Little Guides for almost a century.

The one person who has stood by me and the series longer than Jennifer is my agent, Doris Michaels. She's the only agent I've ever had, and that is quite unusual in the business. We've become good friends from opposite ends of the country, and have expanded our adventures around the world. It's a privilege to be represented by Doris, one that I appreciate all the more after a few tenuous moments. To learn more about the Doris S. Michaels Literary Agency, visit **www.dsmagency.com** online. You'll notice many tips from this book in action on the agency website.

# Contents

# A Note About the Web Links

There are dozens of useful resources included in this book, almost all of them online. All Web addresses begin with *http://* and then continue with the specific address. Because all addresses begin with that ugly combination of letters and symbols, I've chosen to leave it off. Instead, every link in these pages gets right to the specific address.

To make it easy for you to find the links, I've made every one bold and underlined **like this**. To get to the Web page, just type exactly what you see bold and underlined into the address field of your Web browser. For example, to get to **www.yahoo.com**, you would type this into your browser:

www.yahoo.com

To get to **store.yahoo.com**, you would type this into your browser:

store.yahoo.com

With that, you're off! Let's go make you some money.

# The Neatest Little Guide to Making Money Online

# 1 Getting Online Can Boost Your Bottom Line

Welcome to the Internet frontier! By designing a unique website and telling the world where to find it, you can direct a piece of online profits into your own bank account. It doesn't take millions of dollars and a slick advertising campaign to make real money. When the Web first became popular, a friend of mine who is a plumber spent weeks building an attractive site that had nothing to do with his plumbing business. I asked why he bothered. He clicked to a page that offered books for sale and told me, "When somebody buys your book here, I make as much off it as you do." Then he turned off the computer. "Plus, I make money while I sleep." Making as much off a book sale as the author while you sleep is the beginning of a great business. Sell a $27 book and keep $4. Do that 125 times in a month and you just made $500. Keep it going and you'll add $6,000 to your annual income *while you sleep*.

This chapter highlights several ways you can make money with a website. The rest of the book provides you with clear steps to make your site the best it can be for your visitors and your own bottom line.

## Simple and Cheap Marketing

Whether you're selling your favorite books like my plumber friend or finding a new client five states away, the Internet makes marketing simple and cheap. It's called the World Wide Web for a reason, mainly that it connects the whole world into a single web of computers. By putting your information on that web, you make yourself and your business available to the world.

The beauty of this setup is that it provides equal access to the huge and the tiny. You've undoubtedly seen the national advertising that companies like IBM have purchased to get you to visit their websites. They're spending millions of dollars. Meanwhile, a woman named Allison Rivers decided that she could make better cookies with organic ingredients and sell them over the Internet. She created **www.allisonscookies.com** and was in business.

Notice the versatility of the Internet. It serves the needs of sprawling corporations and one-woman cookie shops at the same time. Getting to Allison's Cookies is no more difficult than getting to IBM's site. Each one requires a click of the mouse. A functional website and a few key directory listings is all it took for Allison to capture a portion of the business from people who search the Internet for all-natural cookies.

Of course, more people know about IBM than know about Allison Rivers. That's what millions of dollars spent on ads will do for a brand name. But then again IBM has more people on payroll than Allison's Cookies. Heck, IBM probably has more people on payroll than the total number of cookies Allison has baked in her lifetime.

**You Can Sell This with an Oven and a Web Page**

But Allison is not competing with IBM. She's not even competing with Mrs. Fields. She's simply providing wonderful cookies to anybody who cares to try them, and she's doing it with little more than an oven and a Web page. I doubt very much that she expects to achieve the kind of volume that a national bakery chain achieves. She doesn't need to because her costs of doing business are so low. She does not pay for storefronts, employees, brochures, or yellow pages ads.

Before the Internet, what were her options? Direct mail, space ads in publications, radio commercials, and possibly some publicity in trade magazines. Each one is either expensive or time consuming or both. Online, she creates her website one time and gets it listed in the places where those interested in cookies will find it. Whatever money she makes is hers alone. If volume increases enough, perhaps she will hire somebody to help meet demand. She doesn't need IBM revenues or Mrs. Fields cookie volume. She needs only the level of business that will support her personally.

Simple and cheap marketing? You bet. And anybody can do it.

## Sell Products from Other Companies

My plumber friend will never hear from his book-buying customers. He will never touch the books they buy. He will never collect payment from them. Yet, he will make money when they buy my books from his website.

He's selling products through other companies and making a commission off every one. His products are not all books, either. He sells vacations, music, videos, computers, software, Internet marketing services, vitamins, sports gear, magazines, credit reports, and even business communications services. People come to his site for the articles and jokes that he provides, then they end up buying something from a different company by clicking a link that he provides. They get a product they like, the company makes a sale, and my friend gets a cut of the profits.

Think you can't find appropriate products for your site and offer them for sale? Think again. In Chapter 5, you'll learn about twenty leading companies that will help you get started selling their products. You'll also get to know websites that show you the newest affiliate sales programs and which products are hot. You just enroll in the programs you want, add some simple instructions to your site, and watch your commissions add up.

## Sell Your Own Products

If a cut of the profits isn't enough for you, then you can also sell your own products directly and keep all the profit. Allison Rivers sells cookies. My plumber friend sells crafts that his wife makes from their home. An artist friend of mine sells oil paintings. A photographer friend sells lithographs. I even met a guy who sells koi fish for ponds. People order the fish online and they are shipped overnight in plastic-lined crates.

Think you can't handle the programming to sell products online? Think again. In Chapter 6, you'll discover a store that will take care of all technical details and charge you only $10 per month for your first ten products. People visit your site, browse the attached store, and buy what they want. The store collects payment via credit card and deposits it directly into your bank account. You receive the order and ship your products.

## Advertise on Your Site

Once you've gathered a loyal following of people who are interested in the subject of your website, you have a valuable product to sell to advertisers. They want those eyeballs and the spending dollars they control. As long as you restrict your advertising to products and services that interest your visitors, they won't mind seeing the ads. You can add several hundred dollars per month to your income just by running ads on your popular website.

Think you don't have time to find advertisers and maintain a campaign on your site? Think again. In Chapter 8, you'll see that joining an advertising network can provide you with a steady income and little extra work. You just designate space on your site for the ads to run and let the ad networks fill them.

## It All Adds Up

While the Internet probably won't provide you with fabulous wealth like a handful of famous online entrepreneurs, it can certainly bring enough extra income and savings to change your life.

Just add up the few quick examples I've provided in this chapter. Let's say you start a website that sells books, software, and other items while you go about your normal life. I showed earlier that it could make $500 per month, but let's be conservative and assume only $100. You don't ever need to interact with the customer, so the site can just exist with periodic updates and make money while you sleep.

Once that's on autopilot, you concoct a small home-based business like selling cookies or candles or quilts or jars of honey. This requires more involvement than the stand-alone website. You need to create or buy the product, take orders, collect money, and ship the product. Again, let's be conservative and assume a low volume that produces another $100 per month. This site, by the way, can be combined into the same site that you use to sell books. So you're really maintaining only one website.

Now that you have a site that's earning $200 per month getting a fair amount of traffic, you can turn your attention to advertising. It's possible to charge $1,000 per month for highly targeted ads. You could conceivably keep ten or more ads filled at that price, but you probably won't. A more realistic expectation is to start off making an additional $200 per month from advertising.

If I was a shameless marketer, I could add the $10,000 advertising revenue to an inflated $2,000 income from product sales—hey, anything is *possible*—to get a total of $12,000 per month. Technically, you could do it every month, so I could advertise on the back of the book, "Learn how to make an extra $12,000 every month online!"

With apologies to P. T. Barnum for not exploiting America's reading public, I won't do that. You and I both know that few people are going to make an extra $12,000 each month by reading this book.

However, if you add up my conservative income estimates for selling products from other companies, selling your own products, and advertising to your niche audience, you can reasonably expect to see an extra $400 per month after reading this book.

**Your Web Site Could Help Pay for This**

That's not bad. It's enough to pay for a car, move into a nicer home, or invest for a brighter future. Your goal might be to make more than $400 per month, and you will certainly be able to do that. I just prefer to err on the side of caution. Let's walk before we run.

So that's the potential of the Internet. Now let's start putting these strategies to work for you.

# 2 Getting Online

Before you can make any money online, you need to be online. This chapter will get you there. To some, it may seem silly to pause and discuss which computer to purchase, which Internet service provider to choose, and which software works best. To others, this is an absolute necessity. I was shocked to read the other day that even with the Information Age supposedly changing the economy and how we live, only half of American households own a computer.

To those of you in the other half, I offer this quick primer.

## Buying the Right Computer

Computers are affordable these days, and nearly any model is Internet-ready right out of the box. Apple cleverly calls this an "out of box experience." You merely unpack the parts, connect them to each other, plug in the power cord, and you're ready to go.

### Apple or PC?

The age-old battle still rages about whether Apple Macintosh computers or PC-compatible computers are the best bet. I think this discussion has been reduced to two tradeoffs that most can agree upon.

Apple has been using a graphical point-and-click operating system longer than any PC company. Its operating system is still the easiest to use and always a step or two ahead of Microsoft Windows. I chuckle recalling the T-shirt worn by an Apple fanatic when Windows 95 was first released. In bold letters across the front it declared, "Windows 95 = Macintosh 84." And so it seems even today.

However, the PC has been far more commercially successful than the Macintosh, despite the Mac's superiority. That means Mac owners are directly compatible with a smaller base of computers. They are constantly translating files and converting scripts and jumping through various other hoops in an attempt to make their system work with the rest of the world. Mac users also have a smaller selection of software to choose from.

Those are the two biggest face-off arguments for each platform. The Mac is easiest to use, but the PC is used by more people and therefore more compatible and able to run more software.

But guess what? Your personal preference matters more than any of this. The Mac has had to live in a PC world for so long that sharing information from one computer to the next has become fairly straightforward—even from Mac to PC. Then again, the PC has learned so much by coexisting with the Mac that it has become pretty simple to use. Some have even argued that because most of the world uses Microsoft Windows, it is now familiar to a larger percentage of people and therefore simpler for most people to use. That happens to be the case with me. I've used PCs for years and know exactly how to get my work done on one. Switching to a Mac would force me to stop getting work done for a while and learn a new set of procedures.

I suggest that you spend an afternoon in a local computer store clicking around the various computers. Try a Hewlett-Packard. Try an IBM. Try a Sony. When you've become familiar with these and other PC brands, walk across the store and try the Macs.

Whichever feels best to you is the best for you.

# Buying by Store or Mail Order

Your next big decision is whether to buy your computer right there in the store or to take a bit of time searching through mail-order catalogs. I've helped many people purchase computers over the years and can see the advantages of each method.

It used to be that you could save a bundle by ordering through the mail. The savings were dramatic. These days, they're tiny if they exist at all. It's hard to believe that the local computer store can sell a full-blown system ready for the Internet and nearly everything else for less than $1,000, but it can and does.

All of my computers have come through the mail. My two favorite companies are Dell (800-999-3355) and Gateway (8[illegible]846-4208). Each offers outstanding systems, low prices, and phone support. I suggest that you contact each company for its latest catalog.

Once you have the mail-order catalogs, you can embark on a shopping trip among your local computer stores. Take along the latest newspaper ads and the mail-order catalogs for price and feature comparisons.

I did this recently with my friend, George. He was buying his first computer, and I fully expected it to be a Dell. It's the brand that I currently use, and I had just received the latest catalog in the mail. So when George asked me what kind of computer to get, I replied, "Buy a Dell."

But a funny thing happened at our local CompUSA. We found ourselves looking at brand-new Hewlett-Packard Pavilions that the store was clearing out for upcoming models. We found a Pavilion that offered every feature George needed and, much to my surprise, at a price cheaper than Dell's comparable model. To further tip the scales, CompUSA extended a six-month same-as-cash deal so that George wouldn't need to pay a dime to take his new system home. Finally, there were no shipping charges to pay.

**The Best Deal Might Be Right Up the Street**

In the end, we packed the HP Pavilion into the car and hooked it up back at George's place. I still receive Dell's catalogs and am still happy using my Dell, but the shopping trip with George opened my eyes to the deals available just up the street.

It's probably the same up your street too, so take some time to request catalogs and drive around town comparing computers.

## Buying by Internet

"Wait a minute," you say. "Shouldn't I be able to find the best deals of all by shopping on the Internet? That's what this book is all about."

True, but if you're shopping for a computer then you probably don't have access to the Internet yet. Even if you can get access through a friend or work or the local library, you should still spend time shopping among catalogs and local stores the way George and I did. Computers are not like books. When you buy *The Neatest Little Guide to Stock Market Investing* at Amazon.com, it's the exact same book that you would buy at Barnes & Noble or Borders or your favorite independent bookseller. Aside from price, there's no comparison shopping required.

With computers, there is a difference. George simply preferred the feel of the HP keyboard over competing models. Also, the HP included nifty features like a speaker volume control knob right on the keyboard and quick buttons to take him directly to his favorite Internet sites. To be honest, I began feeling a little jealous because my computer doesn't have those features. I still have to reach across my desk to the speaker volume knob to adjust my sound level.

So I'd hate to see you conduct all your computer shopping over the Internet, where you just see a tiny picture of the computer, a feature list, and a price. You'll eventually be using the real thing, not a thumbnail photo. You need to spend a little time in front of real computers so that you know what you like.

After you've done that, you can certainly check for better deals online. For instance, George might have been able to find the HP Pavilion at a better price online than at CompUSA. As it turned out, he couldn't. Nor could he get the six-month same-as-cash deal. I went home and checked for him and also checked to see if the new Dells offered any keyboard volume control knobs. They didn't.

Here are several online computer stores to check once you know what you like:

- **www.buycomp.com** This is the computer division of Buy.com, one of the most popular shopping sites on the Internet.
- **www.computers.com** Cnet is an objective third party that runs this site, evaluating every available computer and peripheral to help you make the right choice. When you've got a winner, one click takes you to the manufacturer's site to purchase your new system.
- **www.microwarehouse.com** You'll find PCs, Macs, peripherals, books, and everything else you'd expect at this one-stop computer shop.
- **www.onsale.com** The slogan promises smart deals online at cost. The "at cost" part is the attractive part.
- **www.outpost.com** Outpost.com was recently voted the number one hardware store on the Web by the users of TopTenLinks. The store's claim to fame is that it offers free overnight shipping within the United States.
- Finally, don't forget to try the two direct sales kings. Visit **www.dell.com** and **www.gateway.com** to see how well they compete.

## Two Buying Tips

Whether you purchase your computer at a store, through the mail, or over the Internet, here are two simple guidelines to keep the price down on this purchase and to avoid being instantly outdated.

First, buy the almost-fastest machine. The top of the line is much more expensive than the machine that was the fastest just three months ago. Don't get the 1000 megahertz chip, get the 900. If you're convinced that you need the 1000, don't buy it until the 1100 is released with great fanfare. For most users, computers became plenty fast years ago. Take my profession, for example. I'm a writer. The wait time happens in my head—not inside the computer—and so far, I've had no luck upgrading.

Second, make sure the hardware is easily upgradable. What

is a fast modem today will be a snail in one year. What is a huge hard drive today will be tiny in one year. Be sure you can swap out the old and pop in the new improved components as you need them. Notice, as you *need* them, not as the ads tell you that you should have them. If your "tiny" hard drive can still hold everything you need to put on it, there's no need to triple the size. By being able to upgrade your computer one part at a time as necessary, you postpone the very costly purchase of an entirely new system. Apple Macintosh computers include a swing-open side door that makes upgrading as easy as it gets. Some PCs offer the same feature, but once again, not as elegantly as the Mac.

## Don't Expect Tech Support

Let me put it to you straight: the days of decent telephone tech support have vanished. Almost all companies have converted to an Internet-based support system that is hopelessly discouraging. You're better off calling a local computer consultant and paying a few bucks. Not for every little problem, of course, but for anything major.

When you call phone support either for your computer or software you're running, you will be told by a recorded voice speaking in tones that are much too sweet to appreciate in your current crisis that you should visit the company's website. There, the voice promises, you'll find all the answers to frequently asked questions.

Sure, if you have about five hours to fish through every completely unrelated problem and its unintelligible solution, the frequently asked question page is the answer for you. Otherwise, don't bother.

Even if you decide to hold the telephone support line for an hour waiting for the only representative there to take your call, I would bet my last floppy disk that you won't get your problem taken care of. For some reason, today's support people don't know anything about computers. What they do know is a list of inane questions that never apply to you such as, "Is your computer plugged in?" If your computer is plugged in, the representative will then assume that your problem can be better fixed by some other company whose product you're using.

If you're calling Microsoft about Windows, you can be sure that the support person will tell you to call the company that publishes the software application you're using. If you're silly enough to believe that advice and you actually call the software application company and wait on their support line for an hour, you will be told that the problem lies in a little known cavern deep within Windows. "But," you reply through clenched teeth, "I just got off the phone with Microsoft and they said to call you."

Bewilderment ensues. The support person will be aghast that Microsoft would have ever suggested such a solution. After clicking on the keyboard and putting you on hold for several minutes to make it look like a solution to your problem is being pursued, the support person will get back on the line and tell you with all sincerity that you need to contact the computer manufacturer. You realize as you hang up the receiver that a solution to your problem will not be coming over the telephone. It's just you and the computer. Your blood pressure will slowly drop to its normal levels as you carry the machine to the back porch and send it crashing to the rocks below.

If you think I'm kidding about all this, you have never called a support line. It's this bad and far, far worse. So I've got a suggestion for you. Assume from day one that you will never receive any support from any computer company whose product you use. That way, you will not be disappointed. You will seek answers from friends and colleagues at first. Eventually, you will find a reliable consultant in your area who will charge upwards of $50 per hour. Believe me, if anything major goes wrong, you'll be more than happy to pay money for a real human being to show up with a box full of tools and software that will actually fix the problem.

**Here's Where Tech Support Will Get You**

I will grudgingly admit that my proposed solution is exactly what the computer companies hope you'll choose. They provide poor tech support because good tech support is expensive. By providing naive customers with the barest minimum, they can claim on their advertisements that all customers are entitled to free tech support. That makes you feel safe during the purchase, but it's a myth. If truth in advertising ever reaches out to grab the computing industry, products will carry the disclaimer, "Customers who own this product do so at their own risk. In the event of failure, it's everyone for themselves. Good luck."

## Buy a Tape Backup

On that cheery note, I have an important piece of computer shopping advice. Along with your new machine, spend a couple hundred dollars on a tape backup system that's big enough to save your entire computer. Also, buy four tapes.

With this system, you can automate your computer to save a snapshot of all software and data once per week, perhaps every Friday. By rotating the four tapes, you will always have a saved image of everything on your computer for the past month. That way, if you download something off the Internet that explodes your most important application and then pulls out bits of operating system brain, you can just restore the most recent backup tape. If by chance you accidentally backed up an error situation on last Friday's backup, you can go to the previous Friday's backup and so on. You will have four different weeks' worth of backup at any given moment of disaster.

My computer consultant, David Ward, is the one who finally convinced me to get a tape backup. After bailing me out of a close call, he insisted that it was not sufficient for me to just back up my data. Up to that time, I regularly copied my word processor files and other important documents to disks. I thought that was sufficient protection because I could always reinstall the programs and begin using my files after that. I saw no need to backup installed software.

**Get a Tape Backup for Days Like This**

But when my computer crashed one afternoon, the data backups didn't matter a bit. Sure I had my work files, but I couldn't get to any of them because the software applications didn't work. It was like having a backup car with no gasoline. David was able to fix the computer over the weekend, but he said that with a tape backup and a full system snapshot,

I could have been completely restored in about two hours. That's a lot of time and worry I would have saved.

Take it from me. It's worth the money for a complete system tape backup. If you're serious about making money online, then you're operating a business. Just as a store carries fire insurance, your computerized business should carry data insurance.

## Selecting an Internet Service Provider

Once you have your new computer system at home, connected, and plugged in, it's time to choose an internet service provider, abbreviated ISP. That's the company that will provide you with software to dial onto the Internet and a list of phone numbers for your computer modem to dial. The current monthly cost is around $20 for either unlimited usage or enough hours so that for all but the most fanatical Internuts it's the same as unlimited. A certified nerd friend of mine complained one day when his ISP changed from unlimited use to 250 hours per month.

"Richard," I pointed out. "That's more than eight hours a day!"

"I know," he replied. "Who can limit themselves to only eight hours a day?"

Don't be like Richard. You'll probably do fine with 100 or 150 hours. Most of the work you'll do on your website will happen when you're not connected to the Internet. You need to connect only for file uploads, which take very little time. As for using the Internet to browse for information, I have never felt restricted by my plan which gives me 100 hours per month for $20.

**Eight Hours a Day Is Enough**

The much more important consideration in choosing an ISP is the reliability. Some of their lines are busy half the day. Others don't route e-mail to you quickly enough. Still others are so riddled with technical problems that you never seem to have a smooth entry and exit from the Internet.

Your new computer probably came bundled with a few ISPs

such as America Online. You receive a free trial period that you can activate immediately. You'll supply your credit card number but it won't be charged for a month. Go ahead and register with whatever ISP is offered on your new computer so that you can get on the World Wide Web. Once you're able to get online, you may want to shop around a bit to make sure you're with the best ISP. Maybe you'll decide to use America Online or whichever company came bundled with your computer. In that case, you're all set!

On the off chance that you want something else, here are my suggestions in order of preference. Visit the sites for more information and to download their software to get started.

- **www.ibm.net** IBM is known for its reliability in the computing world, and its Internet service lives up to the reputation. The phone lines are rarely busy, the e-mail is delivered quickly, and the dialing software offers a number of nifty customizations. This is the service that I use and I've been quite happy with it.
- **www.att.net** AT&T WorldNet is a good alternative to IBM. It boasts one of the largest networks available and has proven reliable and fast in national surveys.
- **www.earthlink.net** Earthlink has one of the best start pages around. Its access is quick and its e-mail is reliable.
- **www.mindspring.net** Mindspring is known for its user-friendliness. It has a neat feature called Spaminator that blocks *spam*, online jargon for junk e-mail. Again, the connection is fast and reliable. In the company's own words, Mindspring's engineers will be your "geeks in shining armor."
- **www.webisplist.com** If you don't want one of the national ISPs, consider getting a local one. WebISPList is a great place to search your area code for a number of providers in your town. You can see their monthly charges and the usage that's included. In a matter of minutes, you'll find something you like.

Look over the various offerings, then choose an ISP that seems like a good fit. As an enticement, many will offer you free storage space to build a website. Don't spend a lot of time comparing that feature from one company to the next. You're going to build a business website and find a different company called a hosting service to store your files for anyone to view. Right now, you're just looking for the best way to get on the Internet, not to store your website.

If you decide to sign up with an ISP different than the one that came bundled on your computer, be sure to cancel your free subscription to the bundled ISP. If you forget to do so, you'll pay two monthly fees once the free trial period has expired.

# Choosing a Web Browser and an E-mail Program

You already used the web browser that's bundled with your computer to go from one ISP site to the next. The two most popular browsers are Microsoft Internet Explorer and Netscape Navigator, both available for free. You might want to download the browser that you're not using to compare features. Visit **www.microsoft.com/ie** for Internet Explorer and **www.netscape.com/download** for Navigator. They run neck and neck on features and show pages in pretty much the same way. Your personal preference should guide you to choosing one over the other.

Next, it's time to select an e-mail program. You'll find that e-mail is the most important part of getting online. Your customers will communicate with you via e-mail, you will network with others using e-mail, and your vendors will update you with product announcements sent over e-mail. You may find yourself spending more time in your e-mail program than any other software. That being the case, you need to select a program that is easy for you to use. There are several to choose from.

America Online's popular service includes an integrated e-mail program. It pops up as soon as you dial in and speaks the message "You've got Mail" that inspired the movie starring Tom Hanks and Meg Ryan. While AOL's e-mail capabilities are simple to use, they're not very powerful. People who communicate a lot by e-mail usually choose a dedicated e-mail program.

Still, for your first foray into the land of e-mail, AOL will probably be fine. You can always change later.

The most popular stand-alone e-mail program for sale is Eudora. There are people fanatical about this program who consider anything else inferior. It offers a slew of filters, automatic response tools, and a text-to-voice service that reads your e-mail to you over any Touch-Tone phone. There is a free version of the program called Eudora Light, which you can download from **www.eudora.com**. The full-featured Eudora Pro runs about $40. Cnet highly recommended Eudora by describing it as "the Ferrari of e-mail applications."

Both the Microsoft Internet Explorer and the Netscape Communicator browser suites include e-mail programs. Microsoft's is called Outlook Express, Netscape's is called Messenger. They're both up to the task and boast industry awards for simplicity. They leapfrog each other in functionality from one version to the next, but became more than adequate years ago. These programs are included when you download the browser suites.

When you chose your ISP, you also chose an e-mail address. If you're on America Online and chose "my-email," then your address would be "my-email@aol.com." If you ever leave AOL, your e-mail address would change and cause all sorts of trouble as people try contacting you.

To solve this, there are a number of free Internet-based e-mail services that establish a lifetime address and allow you to send and receive e-mail from any computer with access to the Web. The top ones are **www.bigfoot.com**; **mail.yahoo.com**; **www.hotmail.com**; **www.juno.com**; and **www.usa.net**. Even if you sign up with a free e-mail service, you should still use one of the three e-mail programs mentioned above because you need to be able to save and sort messages on your own computer. Hotmail is owned by Microsoft, so its service works closely with the Outlook Express e-mail program.

Another reason you can skip the Internet e-mail services is that you'll create a lifetime e-mail address when you build your Web site later in the book. For example, my e-mail address is jkelly@jasonkelly.com. No matter which ISP I use, that address will always work because it simply points to wherever I currently get online. You'll have a similar address with your website.

The easiest and free way to get your browser and e-mail needs taken care of is to choose between the Microsoft Internet Explorer suite and the Netscape Communicator suite. I've used both and like them a lot.

# Finding the Information You Need Online

Finding information online is easy. Finding the right information online is hard. This section will help you get what you're looking for.

## To the Forest, Then to Your Tree

The Internet provides too much information to find specific documents in a single search. Often you'll type in your query and be presented with thousands of sites to check. After a few hours of that, you'll eventually decide that you didn't really need to know the answer anyway. Maybe a nice hike through the woods is a better use of your time.

That's almost always true, but let's say that you do indeed want to find your answer on the Internet. Instead of trying to get it in one single search, you need to conduct at least two searches. The first one gets you into the right forest, and the second one gets you to your tree. You first want to find the sites that contain the specific pages you're looking for.

To find the sites, use one of the major search engines or directories. The biggies are **www.altavista.com**; **www.excite.com**; **www.hotbot.com**; **www.infoseek.com**; **www.lycos.com**; and **www.yahoo.com**.

Let's say that in researching your business idea you want to know the median family income in your area. Try typing "median family income" into any of the search engines and you'll find more than 5,000 hits dominated by banking and real estate companies. That's way too many and not very useful.

Instead, you need to find the site that will give you the information. Who is it that counts things like median family income?

The Almanac people maybe, probably some encyclopedias, definitely county offices, and the U.S. Census Bureau. Those are the forests, if you will, that contain the tree you're looking for.

Type "census bureau" into Yahoo. Right at the top of its result list is a link to the U.S. Census Bureau site at **www.census.gov**. There you find a search button, then a link to search places. You type in your zip code and are presented with nearly every statistical measurement pertaining to your town. There among them is a document called "median family income." Voilà!

Yahoo is the best place to find dominant sites like the U.S. Census Bureau. It's hand indexed, meaning that human beings have classified the sites into a system like the one at your local library. I find that much more useful than a computer-generated list of every site that contains the phrase you're searching for.

Another good human-driven directory is at **www.about.com**. Type "census bureau" there and you'll get to the U.S. Government Info/Resources page that's maintained by a fellow named Robert Longley as of this writing. Presumably, Robert has spent a great deal of time scouring the Internet for all the pertinent government info that he thinks will be of interest to you. Looking down the list, I'd say he's done a good job.

## Keep Your Own Directory

As you conduct research on all sorts of topics, you'll find your favorite sites. The more you search the longer your list of favorite sites will become. After a while they're hard to remember.

That's why both Internet Explorer and Netscape Navigator provide you with the ability to bookmark your favorite sites. You can also group them into folders and subfolders so that you can easily find them again.

For example, my bookmark list includes a folder called Web Business. Under that are subfolders called Content, Marketing, Transactions, and so on. If I'm writing an article for my website, I will spend time in the Content folder clicking from site to site for ideas and research. If I want to promote my website, I will go to the Marketing folder to see the latest tips at my favorite online marketing and publicity sites. When poking around the Internet, I will occasionally run across a site that I think I'll visit again. If so, I figure out where in my bookmark directory it fits and save it.

Take some time to maintain a well-organized bookmark list. It will become your ultimate directory to the Internet because it will contain exactly the information that's important to you, no searching required.

# 3 Making Business Connections

When you've completed the process of getting online, you should establish yourself so that others can find you. It doesn't take a website to do that. All it takes is a listing in key online communities and a bit of time in appropriate discussion groups and message boards. From those contacts, you will begin sending and receiving e-mail that can lead to lots of business.

## Participating in Online Communities

An online community is a place where people with similar interests gather to exchange information. That's a very broad definition and there are thousands of websites that fit the bill. With most, you sign up by completing a profile form. Other people can then find you and contact you.

### Sixdegrees.com and ICQ.com

The most successful personal networking site of all is **www.sixdegrees.com**, so named because everybody on the planet supposedly knows each other through only six degrees of separation. That's not as intimate as it sounds, however, because six degrees is a lot. It could mean, for instance, that you and I know each other because my sister went to college with a woman who met a guy at her summer internship who once had dinner with a lady who works in the same office as your mother who, we can only hope, knows you rather well. This connection between you and me is tenuous at best and pretty much worthless in most situations. If we sat next to each other on a plane, we wouldn't even know we were connected.

But all that changes online. Suddenly, if I can trace through those flimsy connections and see that you work for a company that buys something I sell, we have a reason to communicate. We probably don't even care why we know each other; we're just glad to have the ingredients in place for a transaction that can benefit both of us.

That is the entire philosophy behind Sixdegrees.com. It looks at where you went to school, where you work, where you live, and who you know to keep track of your degrees of connection to people. Those in your first degree are the ones that you know directly like your colleagues, friends, and family. Those in your second degree are the people that your colleagues, friends, and family know. Those in your third degree are the people that those in your second degree know, and so on through all six degrees.

**Jump into the Big Cloud**

You can specify how much of your personal information is viewable by people in the various degrees so that somebody in the "big cloud," which is what Sixdegrees.com calls the entire site full of connected people, doesn't notice that you live up the street and decide to stop by for a surprise visit. There are other kinds of networking sites for that, which I won't be covering in this book.

Sixdegrees.com is a sort of clubhouse with more rooms than you can immediately see. The more time you spend bouncing around the site the more you'll find to be useful. With over 2.2 million members as of this writing, you are bound to find somebody worth knowing. Here's the site's own summary of its features:

> You can post bulletin board messages to your friends, your friends' friends and your friends' friends' friends; chat live with members from around the world; build and participate in special-interest groups; interview fascinating celebrities; reunite with long-lost friends; send instant degreemail to any sixdegrees member; find out who's logged on and learn more about them through their personal zoom screen; and, best of all, make new friends, network, connect and have a great time while you're doing it.

That pretty much says it all. The site is free, so there's no excuse for not going there and jumping into the big cloud.

Another good networking site is **www.icq.com**. It groups people into "rings" of common interest, like family, sports, and travel. You can create your own interest groups as well. Between e-mail, bulletin boards, chat rooms, and a cool program that tells you when friends and colleagues are online, ICQ is a smart way to get and stay connected.

## People and Business Directories

There are other sites that specialize in connecting you with specific people that you're looking for, as opposed to anybody who might be of help. Such sites are usually called directories. They aren't nearly as full-featured as Sixdegrees.com. They are still useful, however, because a relatively small percentage of the people online have registered at Sixdegrees.com while the directories use phone books and public records to list people whether they know it or not.

The five major directories are **www.555-1212.com**; **www.anywho.com**; **www.bigbook.com**; **www.infospace.com**; and **www.switchboard.com**. Also, each of the major search engines listed on page 19 offers people and business directories. Of all these choices, Anywho is my favorite. Created by the Internet Directory Group of AT&T Labs, it offers the most powerful search capabilities and a simple way to add, change, or remove your own listing. Take a moment to search for yourself. If you're not listed, add yourself and your business. If you are listed, make sure the information is accurate.

## Keep Your Information Current

It's important to keep your information current at Sixdegrees.com, directories, and other online communities. Some directories don't allow you to change your listing because they pull it from existing sources. So the only way to keep current there is to make sure that your listing in phone books is accurate. You probably do that anyway.

You can lose your mind trying to keep your listing up to speed everywhere. I suggest that you always keep your Sixdegrees.com listing accurate. That's the most important one because you will actively participate in that community. After that, keep a bookmark folder called "Directories" and put your favorite directories in it. Occasionally, take half an hour to go to each one and search for yourself. You'll probably be listed accurately and can then forget about it for a few months.

Don't spend too much time on the directories. They're nothing more than a new version of the phone book. Just as you don't get a ton of business phone calls from your listing in the white pages, don't expect to get a ton of business e-mail from your listing in online directories. Remember, we're all eventually going to be in there. Your name among hundreds of millions of others is not especially noticeable. Just make sure that when somebody who really wants to do business with you tries to find you, they can do so easily.

# Participating in Message Boards

One of the most effective ways to communicate with and learn from groups of people online is a message board. You post messages to the group and read messages from the group. The messages are usually grouped by topic and the discussions that follow are called "threads." For instance, if I posted a message with the subject "making money online," all replies to the message would be collected together into the "re: making money online" thread. That way, it's easy for you and others to focus on only the information of interest to you.

You need to register with a board before you can post messages. Most allow you to read messages posted by others whether you've registered or not. When you finally get the urge to add your two-cents' worth, you'll need to tell the board a little about yourself, supply your e-mail address, and choose a name that you'll be known by. It can be your real name if it hasn't been taken, or one that you make up like Osprey or LittleHero or DragonLady. Choose carefully because once you're known by your board name there's no going back. If you don't want to forever be addressed as SlimeBaby, then choose something else.

There are millions of message boards. You will often find them at the sites that you use everyday. If you're in the investment business, you'll find tons of investment message boards at sites like **www.fool.com** and **www.ragingbull.com**. If you're a traveler, try **www.frommers.com**. I could go on forever, but you get the point. Message boards are just about anywhere that people with common interests gather.

When you're trying to expand your circle of contacts or promote your business, message boards are excellent tools for two reasons: first, because they can provide you with valuable information; second, because when you provide others with valuable information, those people are likely to keep in touch with you. All contact is an opportunity to conduct business.

Let's say that you sell homemade quilts and have decided to take your business to the Internet. You want to know more about the online quilting community, so you conduct a search at Yahoo on "quilting business message boards."

You find a number of suggested sites, but none that look more promising than About.com's at **quilting.about.com**. On the message board, you read posts about quilting classes and labels on baby quilts that bleed ink when the baby spits up on them. That gets your juices flowing about making money from your online quilting store, and you click the button to post your own message. You ask if anybody can point you to a few good resources for marketing a quilting business on the Internet. You check back a few days later and find several responses. That's the right way to use a message board.

Now, the entirely wrong way to use a message board would be to post something like this:

> I just took my world-famous quilting business to the Internet. Stop by to see me at www.worldfamousquilts.com where you can order the best quilts on the planet. You don't feel comfortable ordering online? Then call our toll free number at 1-800-339-5671 where we accept every credit card and ship the same business day. Call NOW!

**Don't Abuse the Message Boards or You'll Be Attacked**

A post like that will get you blacklisted in no time. The board supervisor will probably delete the post and send you a reprimanding e-mail. If other board readers see it first you will likely get *flamed*, which is the word for being deluged by hateful e-mails telling you that you're not worth the air you breathe. Message boards are not intended for blatant commercial advertising. Make sure that you don't try to use them that way.

However, there would be nothing wrong with a post along these lines:

> I understand the trouble with babies spitting up on labels and smearing the ink. I found a wonderful way to solve that problem by using my new baby-proof inkjet paper that you can use right on your home computer printer. It's a snap to use and will never run. Be sure to reverse the image of the label when you print it so it'll read correctly after you iron the transfer onto the fabric. If you want to know more about the paper, please visit my website at www.worldfamousquilts.com. I hope this helps.

You should be able to see the difference immediately. Both messages point readers to your website, but the first one does so with no helpful information attached. It's just a typed commercial that you were able to post for free on a community message board. The second post answers a fellow board-reader's problems with ink running on labels. That's useful information. What's more, you happen to sell a product that will solve the person's problem. Such specific and low-profile promotions are fine. They're done all the time, and nobody minds because they're consistent with the message board's mission to provide readers with a forum for giving and receiving useful information.

To get your feet wet in a few message boards, visit **boards.excite.com**; **boards.lycos.com**; and **messages.yahoo.com**. Each provides boards on hundreds of topics. But remember that the truly great message boards are featured at sites specializing in a single area of interest like investing, travel, quilting, or home lizard care. Search for the best sites in your interest area and you'll find the best boards.

## Participating in Chat Rooms

Most chat rooms are worthless for business. They gather people together online where they can fire meaningless comments back and forth to each other. The very fact that the people have nothing better to do than stare at their computer screens waiting to see an inside joke between two other people they've never met should tell you something about the quality of information you can expect to receive. It's low, the worst of pop culture and porn and teen malaise.

Before I continue, let me explain how a chat room works. It's similar to a message board except that nothing is saved for future viewing. You don't read a message that somebody posted last Tuesday. You log into the chat and view quips and comments that somebody typed ten seconds ago. When there are dozens of people in the chat, these comments can come in rapid-fire procession. The chats are usually organized around a specific topic, but good luck finding anybody who's capable of sticking to the topic.

As with message boards, you'll need to register before you can participate in a chat room. Some services like Yahoo use one registration for all message boards and chat rooms. To see rooms in action, stop by **chat.yahoo.com** and **www.chatcom.com**. They are among the cleaner destinations.

**Don't Waste Your Time in Chat Rooms**

You would think there might be business chat rooms where professionals could congregate for the purpose of exchanging helpful information, but I haven't found any. Something happens to otherwise professional people when they enter a chat room. They can't resist tossing out a quip about the president even though you're in a marketing chat room. Each inane quip begets five or six more quips as people try to out-silly the next person. Before long, the entire focus of the chat room is lost. That being the case, people will start leaving the chat room. Then a whole new group will arrive. A few words about marketing will be provided, then somebody will make a quip about Austin Powers and the runaway train will careen once again.

If that scenario fails to unfold, then you'll be met with a group of people who do nothing but chat all day long and therefore know each other better than their own families. They will repeat yesterday's jokes as if reminiscing about the good ol' days in college. Everyone but you will get the biggest kick out of seeing each other's typed reaction all over again. Ah, the progress of technology.

Lest you think I'm exaggerating, here's a real excerpt from a chat room about small business marketing:

> MOREY: where did you go?
> XTAR3: to get a drink
> WALLA: hello quixa. long time no see
> EMERALDS1999: data dump!
> QUIXA: lol--hi walla!!!!!!!
> SOME_DWEEB: you guys suck
> WALLA: rotflol. how's business?

Now, wasn't that time well spent? Let's see, we know that XTAR3 grabbed a drink and that MOREY missed him while he was away. We know that WALLA and QUIXA find each other quite funny and are tickled pink that they can once again exchange funny abbreviations like LOL for "laughing out loud" and ROTFLOL for "rolling on the floor laughing out loud." We have no idea what EMERALDS1999 is attempting to communicate. We can probably agree with SOME_DWEEB, who thinks everybody in the room sucks. That includes us at the moment, so we head for the exits as quickly as possible, vowing to never again enter a chat room.

If you stick to the vow in that last sentence, then I've accomplished my goal in this section. Chat rooms are not about business, they're about killing time. The people in there have nothing better to do. Hopefully, you do have something better to do. Taking a walk in the park would be better for your business.

There are extremely rare exceptions to the way I've characterized chat rooms. They are so rare in fact, that I consider them to be statistical discrepancies. If you need to see a chat room for yourself, just remember that I warned you. Escape is never more than a click away.

## Participating in Newsgroups

You have to check message boards for the latest information and you have to watch chat rooms to see the discussion taking place. If neither of these options is appealing to you, perhaps a newsgroup will work better. It's like a message board with people from everywhere posting. However, instead of being displayed at a website, each post is displayed on your computer through your e-mail program's newsgroup feature.

Collectively, newsgroups and the people who use them are called Usenet. It's not an organization or a software program or even a set of standards maintained by anybody. Usenet is just the combined mass of users all communicating with each other through newsgroups. Occasionally, a user will become annoyed with the conduct of another user and write, "this forum is not supposed to be treated this way." To which somebody else will almost always reply, "says who?"

Newsgroups are organized by the name of their subject, which might be alt.society.revolution or rec.arts.poems. The prefix "alt" stands for alternative and "rec" stands for recreation. Other common prefixes include "biz" for business, "comp" for computing, "misc" for miscellaneous, "sci" for science, and "soc" for society.

These cryptic names are not typed into your browser like a Web address, but selected from a list that you get from your e-mail program. To learn more about your program's specific newsgroup features, search the online help for "newsgroups." Subscribing to groups is usually as simple as going to the newsgroup section of your e-mail program, pushing a button to download the latest available groups, looking over the names, viewing some of the sample posts, then subscribing to the groups of interest to you.

After you're subscribed, you will receive posts from the group whenever you push the "synchronize" or "update" button in your e-mail program's newsgroup section. Some programs allow you to specify automatic updating of the list periodically. You read the posts exactly as you read your e-mail. You have the choice of creating a new post with your own subject heading, replying only to the author of an existing post, or replying to the entire newsgroup.

When you begin using newsgroups, be sure to create a profile for yourself that includes beneficial business information. For example, display the name of your company along with your website. This is not intrusive at all. People expect to be able to reach you if you're posting to a newsgroup. If you list your website, curious readers will be able to easily go there to see what you're all about.

Some newsgroups are moderated, meaning that all posts are sent to a moderator for approval before getting broadcast to the group. Moderated newsgroups filter out much of the clutter that plagues online communications. When HappyBart from Chillicothe decides to send "What's up, dudes?" to the group, the moderator will kindly spare you the distraction.

To see lists of newsgroups organized into categories, visit **www.cyberfiber.com**; **www.deja.com**; and **www.newsville.com**.

## Getting the Most from E-mail

When you've made connections with people through networking sites, message boards, and newsgroups, those people will want to stay in touch with you by e-mail. You're already prepared for that because you chose an e-mail reader on page 18. Here are four tips for sending e-mail messages that don't anger the people receiving them.

## Always Personalize

The mass marketers of the world nearly giggled themselves silly when they first encountered e-mail. Just think, they could send solicitations to millions of people instantaneously without spending a dime to do it. It seemed almost too good to be true.

It was. People are so fed up with junk e-mail that they've begun using filters to send most of it immediately to their DELETE folder.

You can learn a lot about what's important to people by examining the filters they use to identify such e-mail. Do they automatically throw away all notes containing the words "get rich" or "you've already won"? No. Do they automatically throw away notes sent by a certain junk e-mail house? No. The most common junk e-mail filter people teach their computer is this: Discard all notes that do not have my real name or my e-mail address in the address field. Say your name is Walt Wilson and your e-mail address is walt@wilson.com. If a note arrives without "Walt Wilson" or "walt@wilson.com" in the address field, your computer will automatically discard the note.

You'd be amazed at the effectiveness of this quick filter. Millions of e-mail notes are sent everyday with the words "list1," "recipients," or "customer" in the address field. Such an impersonal approach screams junk so clearly that a robot blocking junk mail can trash the message before it ever gets opened. It's the equivalent of receiving regular postal mail addressed to "Current Resident." Why bother with the formality at all? They should just use "Human with Money."

The lesson for you is to always personalize your e-mail. If five different people e-mail you about the quilt you're selling from your website, you might be tempted to group all of their names together and send a note that begins "Dear Friend." Remember that people want to see their name on their e-mail. Even if you send the exact same response to all five inquirers, take the time to copy it into five separate notes, begin each one with the recipient's name, and send each of the five individually to their destinations.

**Personalized E-mail Gets Noticed**

Too time consuming, you say? It isn't for Amazon.com. The company sends a personalized response to everybody e-mailing for help. There's no autoresponder spending the night mass e-mailing an answer to every inquiry containing certain words. A human being reads the incoming e-mail and then responds to the sender with information specific to the situation. If personalized e-mail is important enough to one of the busiest Internet companies, it's important enough to you.

Use people's names and tailor your notes to them directly. The extra care will pay off for years to come.

## Keep It Short but Complete

When you take up somebody's time with an e-mail message, make sure you do so respectfully. To me, that translates into keeping your notes as short as possible but providing complete information so that the recipient can take immediate action.

Here's the conclusion to a lengthy note sent to me by a colleague. It serves as an example of how e-mail should *not* be written:

> So, anyway, that's just what I've been thinking about and we can't come to a final decision yet but I thought I'd run it by you. There's not much more you can add at this point except to know that I'll send you all the details when they're available. Maybe then we can get together and make a decision.

Why bother sending a note that ends like this one? If there's nothing I can do, why the heck was I forced to read the lengthy details as they exist today? Venting, I suppose. My colleague wanted to do something with all the thoughts running through his mind, so he performed a brain dump into an e-mail note and fired it off to me. Now I'm the poor sap who has to read the whole novelette because my colleague was too inconsiderate to wait until there was enough information for me to actually help solve the problem.

Make sure you have something to say to people before you start communicating with them. We all have limited time and limited attention spans. If you receive three worthless, lengthy notes from me, how eager are you going to be to open the fourth note from me? Not very. All bad notes are like crying wolf. They create an atmosphere that renders your truly important notes ineffective because none of the recipients take you seriously anymore.

**Don't Bore People to Death**

Give people just the information they need, but all the information they need. You'll spend less time spewing useless e-mail and your recipients will appreciate spending less time reading useless e-mail.

## Provide Complete Contact Info

You want people to be able to get in touch with you as easily as possible. A quick way to accomplish that is to add the details of your business card at the bottom of every e-mail you send. Your e-mail program will even allow you to save the information into a "signature" that's automatically added when you send a note. For example:

---

Amanda B. Reckonwith
Marriage Counselor
**amanda@reckonwith.com**
**www.reckonwith.com**
7777 Reckonwith Road
Los Angeles, CA 90065
333-444-0002 FAX
333-444-0001 TEL

---

Online, the e-mail address and Web address are hyperlinked so people can just click on them to send a note or visit the website. It's all plain, unformatted text including the horizontal divider lines, which are just underscore marks strung together. You can create those by pressing the "shift" and the "-" keys on your keyboard together.

Keeping everything in plain text is a good idea, by the way.

Some people try to get fancy by adding graphics and animation, and even sound to their notes. Don't do that.

First of all, it annoys most people to stumble into a circus act when all they expected was a few paragraphs of text. Second, not all e-mail readers can display fancy attachments. There's a good chance that half or more of your recipients won't see anything but funny symbols at the bottom of your notes. All e-mail readers can handle plain text. Third, fancy attachments can make notes big in size so that it takes longer to download them from the mail server to your recipient's computer; plus they will take up more space once they've arrived there. People aren't going to be thrilled when a three-megabyte note arrives from you only to communicate that you would like to have lunch.

Nobody wants to be dazzled by your e-mail techno-wizardry. Just give them your intelligent thoughts and complete contact info in plain text.

## Keep Important Contacts in Your Address Book

Over time, you'll come in contact online with hundreds of people who you will want to contact again. Sometimes months will go by without either of you sending a note. Then, one day, there'll be a reason that you want to send a request to the Vice President of Sales at Billionaire Corporation and, gosh darn it, you can't seem to find her e-mail address. You scribbled it somewhere, but now it's gone.

Don't find yourself in this situation. Make a habit of saving every important contact in your e-mail program's address book. It's easy to do. When somebody sends you a note, you can use the menu at the top to add the sender to your address book. A panel will appear where you can modify the information. For instance, you may want to add a note to yourself reminding you that this person is in charge of all new product acquisitions. That way, when you poke around for leads in the future, you'll remember who all the generic-sounding names are.

When you keep your address book current, your circle of influence will grow quickly and you'll be able to surprise people from time to time by dropping a personal note into their reader out of the blue. It can be as effective as sending a card through regular mail, and it will take only a few moments of your time and cost you nothing.

## Respond Promptly

People expect e-mail to be a quick way to communicate. If somebody sends you a note on Monday, they probably expect to hear back from you by Wednesday and definitely by Friday. Sending a note to somebody who takes two weeks to respond is discouraging.

This is particularly important for customer service. If somebody is asking how they can buy your product, let them know the same day! Better still, make it obvious on your website how they can buy your product. That's a different discussion that will take place later in the book. For now, just remember that you should respond to all e-mail quickly, but especially so in the case of customer service e-mail.

# 4 Creating Your Own Website

At this point, you've got your computer and you've poked around the Web a bit. You've sent and received e-mail. It's time to move on to creating a profit center for yourself in the form of a website that can earn money twenty-four hours a day. It's easy to do, and you can go as fast or as slow as you like.

## Selecting a Website Hosting Service

The first step in establishing a website is finding a place for it to live. A website is just a collection of files that contain the text and pictures that you see on your monitor screen. A hosting service maintains computers that are always connected to the Internet to provide people with access to your files. For example, when you type in **www.jasonkelly.com**, the files I created are read by your browser off the hosting service that I use.

All you need from a hosting service is a fast connection to the Internet, a cheap monthly price, and decent customer service in case there is a problem. If everything is running smoothly, you will never need to deal with your hosting service. All you'll see is a charge on your credit card each month or quarter. That's what you're seeking.

I chose a service called Hostpro in Los Angeles after seeing that big names like Xerox and Baskin-Robbins use the service. Hostpro charges me $19.95 per month for 60 megabytes of storage space. Because most of your pages will be entirely text with just a few pictures thrown in here and there, 60 megabytes should be plenty. To give you an idea, this page of text that you're reading is about 7 kilobytes when turned into an online document. That means you could store 8,571 of these pages before you'd exceed 60 megabytes. If that day ever comes, you can always pay a bit more per month for additional storage space.

The price at Hostpro is about what you should expect to pay for basic service. There's usually a onetime setup fee of around $50 and a monthly fee of around $20. Using those prices as a benchmark, I suggest that you compare the offerings at the following three national hosting services. Each is capable of handling your website with aplomb.

- **www.digiweb.com** Digiweb is always looking for ways to help your website stand out. For instance, their eShare Expressions feature lets you add a chat room to your site. That might keep people coming back. You will use an account manager to make changes to your settings.
- **www.hiway.com** Hiway Technologies offers nifty packages like an express start program that will have you up and running in under an hour using the company's online software. You will have a control panel to adjust settings to your own preferences.
- **www.hostpro.com** Hostpro offers friendly customer support over the telephone, which you'll probably never need because the service just works. That's the highest compliment I can give. Hostpro builds a control panel for your website that shows daily and weekly traffic.

If none of the above three fit what you're looking for, try **www.webhostlist.com**. There you'll find a comprehensive directory of site hosting services ranging from Fortune 500 database-management needs to lemonade-stand online-brochure needs.

When you find a hosting service that fits your plans, either call the toll-free number or fill out the online application to get started. You will provide your credit card number and contact information. The company will send you an e-mail containing details like your initial password and instructions for getting website files from your computer onto the hosting computer.

## Choosing a Domain Name for Your Site

Somewhere during the application for your online hosting account, you'll be asked for your domain name. That refers to the unique Web address that will take people to your site. Yahoo's is www.yahoo.com. Yours might be www.yourname.com.

You need to register your domain name. Your hosting service can do this for you, or you can do it yourself at **www.networksolutions.com**. It's cheaper to do it yourself, and all it takes is typing your name into a field right at the top of the page. The cost to register an address at Network Solutions is currently $70 for the first two-year period. You will then be billed $35 per year after that.

You can choose the typical ".com" ending which stands for commercial use, or you can choose ".net" for Internet-related sites or ".org" for organizations. These initial designations have become blurred as people rush to get their own company name onto the Internet and take whatever is available. In fact, Network Solutions markets a program where you can register your domain name with all three extensions. As you can see, the designations have become fairly meaningless. If your company name is already taken with a ".com" at the end, you might want to try a ".net" instead, although that will probably already be taken as well. The best ending to have is ".com." That's what browser software assumes when somebody types in your company name by itself. For instance, if you type "rafting" you will go to **www.rafting.com**. The Norwegians who own **www.rafting.net** are out of the picture unless somebody types in the entire address. Few people will do so.

Remember that the name you choose for your site will be on everything you use in your business. It's going to show up on

**Get the Most Bang from Your Name**

cards, envelopes, letterhead, product packaging, signs, ball caps, and T-shirts. Make sure you choose a name that you want to see in all those places. Make sure you're proud to tell people your Web address and that they can actually understand what you just said. You may have been listening to a radio program where the host says to visit the website at www.thisisthelongestdarnedsiteaddressinhistoryasfarasiknow.com. Who in the world is going to remember that? Nobody, so it's useless. Even if somebody does manage to scribble that address down, they're going to resent typing a small term paper just to see your site.

Here are some tips to help you come up with a good name:

- Choose one that you like and will continue liking for some time. This seems basic, but I've seen dozens of people roll their eyes in embarrassment when telling me their absurd Web addresses. "Come see my website at, well, I mean it's sort of weird and I might change it soon, but anyway, it's www.whackylulu.com. You see, it was a childhood nickname and I just thought . . ." Is this really how you want to be presenting yourself forever? No. Choose a name you like.

- Choose a name that is flexible enough for you to use no matter where your business goes. A company named "Pink Shoelaces" will do well as long as the only products it ever sells are pink shoelaces. But what if, on a whim, the owner decides to offer yellow shoelaces? Does the business become plain "Shoelaces"? Then what if the company decides to sell socks? You can see where a restrictive name becomes a problem in a hurry. Learn a lesson from Amazon.com. By building a brand name that could mean anything, the company has the freedom to sell books, music, and videos. It can offer shopping services. It can host auctions. It can do just about anything it wants to do at its website and the name still works. Yours should be as flexible.

- Choose a name that is short, easy to say, and easy to spell. People don't like typing long Web addresses. It's tedious and there's lots of room for error. Besides, long names look ugly in Web addresses. You want a short name that rolls off your tongue and that people instantly know how to spell. Again, learn from Amazon.com. It's spelled exactly how it sounds when you say it. It's short and easy to type. By comparison, Waldrof.com is not. It's confusing because it sounds like Waldorf, which is the more common word. You don't know how to spell it when you first hear it. Waldrof could be spelled "Walldrof" or "Waldroff" or even "Walldroff." Why mess with all this?

• Avoid weird characters in your name. The use of dashes, underscores, tildes, and other characters makes Web addresses more difficult. They're harder to remember, much harder to type, and clumsy in spoken communication. "Visit my website at My dash Life dash Story dot com" is not a powerful marketing message. However, the invitation to stop by mylifestory.com is intriguing, assuming it's written by somebody you care about.

• Avoid names that are trendy. The words *cyber* and *virtual* have lost all impact as harbingers of a new age. They now sound cliché. Choose a name that isn't tied directly to the Internet because the newness of the net has already worn off for many people and will do so for everybody else soon. You don't feel special when you place a phone call. You won't feel special visiting a website either, no matter how cool the name seems.

If you're at a complete loss for a good name and don't mind shelling out $30 for a list of 260,000 good, available addresses, visit **www.unclaimeddomains.com**.

# Purchasing Website Design Software

Once you have an account at a hosting service and you've chosen your domain name, it's time to buy the software you need to design your website.

## The Pieces of a Website

A website consists of the text files that display words and pictures on browser screens, programs that are run by the text files, and pictures. There are fancy sites that utilize a wider range of pieces, but for what you want to tackle yourself from home, this is about all there is to it.

In fact, I keep my site even simpler. Mine consists only of text and pictures. That's it. I don't do any special programming. I will occasionally use a program offered for free from another site, but doing so consists only of pointing to it or dropping a chunk of instructions directly into my website. I don't need to keep the program on my computer or maintain it in any way.

This simple two-piece approach that I use restricts my software needs to just one program. I need site design software where I actually lay out the pages and type the text. Some people would add that they need a graphics program where they can create or modify graphics like photos and buttons and banners. However, I consider a graphics program to be optional because so many excellent graphics already exist in ready format. I'm no artist and never expect to be able to create graphics better than the ones already available. Besides, I don't want to. You might feel the same way. If so, you'll do just fine having only a site design program.

## You Don't Need to Know HTML

When you visit a website, your browser reads files that are written in Hypertext Markup Language, abbreviated HTML. The language identifies different elements of the Web page so that your browser knows how to display them. Your word processor does the same thing but you don't see it because it all happens like magic behind the scenes.

For example, when you specify that you want a word printed in **bold**, your word processor actually precedes the word with a character that tells it to begin showing bold text, then follows the word with another character telling it to stop showing bold text. In the early days of word processing, you had to type the special characters yourself. I remember doing so on school papers. Today, of course, you just highlight the word with your mouse and click a button to turn it bold.

Guess what? Creating Web pages has already gone through the same evolution so that you don't need to specify formatting characters anymore. The HTML is done entirely for you behind the scenes. You can spend all of your time designing a good site instead of typing arcane text for a browser to interpret.

## Choosing Your Program

Now that you know the pieces of a website and are comforted by the fact that you don't need to learn any programming to create them, you'll understand what you're looking for in your website design software.

In a word: simplicity. You don't want to become a computer geek just to put helpful information on the Internet. You want to create unique content and a distinctive look and a special place all your own. Well, actually, you hope it doesn't remain all your own. You hope it becomes the most crowded place online. Still, the way to make that happen is through design and content creativity, not nerdiness and hours spent fighting with your computer.

Therefore, you want a program that you barely notice you're using. I've tried many website design programs and watched them improve over the years. The best ones have four features in common:

- *Universal compatibility.* This feature comes with dozens of different brand names like Anywhere HTML and Roundtrip HTML. No matter what it's called, universal compatibility means that the pages you design will work with anybody's browser. That's worthwhile, don't you think?

• *Visual page design.* This is sometimes called WYSIWYG for What You See Is What You Get, which means that the layout you build on your screen is exactly what the page will look like when it's put on the Web. Some software touts this feature by claiming "pixel-point accuracy." Your placement of objects is precise down to a single monitor pixel. If you want a picture over there, drop it and that's where it'll be. If you want text to flow around the picture with a quarter-inch margin, just expand the frame around the picture and it's done. If you want your headline in bold, make it bold on your screen and it'll be bold online. This seems so basic, yet it took years to happen. Don't design without it.

• *Design templates.* Sometimes a little professional help saves you lots of time. Design templates provide you with a collection of buttons, banners, and other elements to give your site an instant theme. Top design software provides you with dozens or hundreds of templates to choose from.

• *Site management.* Sometimes the biggest headache of a large website is just managing all the files and their links back and forth. Site management tools make it easy for you to see what goes where, which pages are linked to each other, which pages aren't linked anywhere, and so on. The simplest way to show this is like a company org chart. Your homepage is at the top, then come the pages directly under it, then the pages under those, and so on. A homepage, by the way, is just the first page of your site. It's the one that people first see when they type your domain name. That's why it goes at the top of your site org chart. Good site management tools allow you to grab any page of your site and drag it to a new location with all of the links still intact.

With these four requirements firmly in place, I have scoured the current offerings. Website design software, also known as authoring software or editing software, has shaken out to a few winners. I chose the following three programs not for their sales volume or advertising campaigns, but because I think they are the best all-around choices for the do-it-yourself site designer. That's you! All three programs are available for Windows and Macintosh, and all three programs sold for $300 at the time of this writing.

- **Dreamweaver** Published by Macromedia, Dreamweaver gives you plenty of room to grow by offering extensions. These add-ons enhance the main program to let you build just about any kind of site you can imagine.
  **www.macromedia.com/software/dreamweaver**

- **GoLive** Published by Adobe, GoLive has an almost fanatical following. It smoothly combines the creative side of design with the technical side of website development. As an added bonus, it is tightly integrated with Adobe's suite of award-winning graphics programs.
  **www.adobe.com/prodindex/golive/main.html**

- **Fusion** Published by NetObjects, Fusion was the first program to offer visual design, and it has maintained its lead to this day. The program's hierarchical site management is so simple that it's hard to believe you're actually changing your site around.
  **www.netobjects.com/products/html/nf4.html**

Those are the big three. You won't go wrong choosing any of them. Whatever Dreamweaver can design, GoLive and Fusion can design as well. Your choice should be based on personal preference. Do you like the interface? Are you able to create a simple page with a few mouse clicks and a couple minutes at your keyboard? Does the program feel suited to your site ideas? The answer to all these questions should be yes.

Of course, you'll be able to choose one only after you've tried all three. Stop by each website and download the free trial versions. Play around with them for a few days and decide which one is best for you. Then return to the website and purchase the program.

I use NetObjects Fusion and have for years. There've been times when it has looked like one of the other two surpassed

Fusion, but not with anything important enough for me to go through the hassle of switching. Besides, Fusion managed to leapfrog the others within a few months. Then they leapfrogged back. That's how it always goes with software—which is exactly why you should choose the one that fits your plans best and stick with it. As long as you can get your work done smoothly, why do you care if you own the product that won the latest shoot-out in a computer magazine? Take it from somebody who's been burned by useless upgrades and switches: You don't.

## Learning to Use Your Program

The best way to learn how to use your new design software is to experiment with it. Go through the tutorial. Make a website that showcases your favorite drinking establishments. Add a line. Drop a button. Link the button to your friend's website. Change the background color. Make a piece of text blink and then promise me that you'll never use that feature in your real business website.

Consider purchasing a how-to book to keep near your computer. These are great to have when you're learning new software because they're often faster than the online help.

My favorite series of how-to software guides are called the *Visual QuickStart Guides* published by Peachpit Press. Most of the text is presented in numbered steps beside screen captures to show exactly where you should be in the program. The topics are arranged by the task you're trying to complete. For example, to create a text frame you would read the section called "How to create a text frame." If this seems difficult to you, I can't wait to see what kind of website you manage to create!

For the *Visual QuickStart Guides* and a listing of other helpful books about Dreamweaver, GoLive, and Fusion, stop by my website. It links you directly to the titles at Amazon.com. You'll learn how to offer this service yourself in Chapter 5.

## Transferring Your Files

After you create or modify the files for your website, which is usually described as authoring your site, you will copy them from your computer to your hosting service. Software tools that help you do this are called FTP programs. FTP stands for File Transfer Protocol. It has become as easy as copying files from your hard disk to a floppy disk. You simply highlight what's on your computer and drag it over to the host computer just as if the host computer was your floppy disk. The files zip through your modem across the phone lines and onto the host computer. You can then open your Web browser and go to your actual live site on the World Wide Web to see your work in action.

As simple as the FTP programs are, your life will be even simpler because you'll never need to use them. Why? Because Dreamweaver, GoLive, and Fusion all offer one-button publishing of your site. That is, FTP is built right into your design software. When you're finished working on your site for the day, you go to the publishing section of the software and push the button to publish your site. You can even specify certain pages if you've worked on only a few. That way the program copies just the changed pages instead of your entire site. It's a real time-saver.

**Transferring Your Files Is Easy**

To use the built-in publishing feature of your design software, you'll need to tell the program some information about your hosting service. It needs to know your remote host address for transferring files. This is usually just ftp.yoursite.com, but I've seen different ones. It also needs to know your base directory for placing files, your account name, and your password.

All of this info is available from your hosting service. If it's not in the initial e-mail the company sent to you, simply e-mail the support team a request for your specific information.

By the way, you only need to tell the design software this information one time. Once it knows where to publish your site and has the necessary password, you just push the PUBLISH button for all future updates.

# Designing Your Site

It's time to design and post your site to the Web. Thanks to your choice of software from among the best three Web design programs on the planet, building a site is going to be about as easy as creating a document in your word processor. Therefore, the challenge lies not in the mechanics of creating your site, but in the artistry and creativity of making it come alive.

## Decide on Your Site's Mission

Why will your website even exist? There are millions of them, soon to be billions, and there doesn't seem to be a reason to add one more. Will it entertain people, inform people, annoy people, or just take up space on a host somewhere? These are important questions.

There are three types of websites:

- *Entertainment.* Glitzy design is the hallmark of entertainment sites. They are usually graphics intensive and sometimes even require special software to view properly. You will often find games, moving pictures, and sounds at entertainment sites.
- *Informational.* Text is the main tool at an informational site. You go there to get certain types of information, and it usually comes in text form. Typical content at an informational site includes news, articles, sports scores, and movie showtimes.
- *Commercial.* Selling is the only reason a commercial site exists. Some sell products through an online catalog, others sell services.

They all borrow a bit from each other, but their prime missions are quite different. For instance, your site will probably provide some form of entertainment or information to visitors, while offering them related products to purchase. That's how my site works. The content keeps people coming back while the products allow me to earn money.

You are starting a Web business and are therefore seeking the same thing. You want to make money by having people purchase items from your website and possibly advertising on your site. In either case, you need traffic. You need eyeballs. You need little mice clicking gleefully from one page to the next. And you need it to happen every day.

Ask yourself how you plan to keep those little mice coming back to click every day. If it's through articles related to the economy, you will want a website that makes it easy to get to the exact information that busy professionals want. If it's to showcase your artwork, you're going to want a beautiful design that brings out the best of your portfolio.

You don't want to create a place for artists that looks like a handout from a tax management seminar. Conversely, you don't want to publish your tax management advice on a site that looks like a colored hotwax accident. You want a site that blends your content with an appropriate design that enables you to make money.

## Keep Your Goals Realistic

I want to warn you right up front that a website can eat up your entire work week if you're not careful. This is true for teams of website workers, so you as a one-person show are even more vulnerable. The challenge for small websites is to keep interesting material changing frequently with as little time spent as possible. Now is when you should begin laying the ground rules that will help you meet that challenge. If you make it part of your site's character from the time you design it, you will have much better odds of succeeding. Here is a handful of pointers to help you maintain a winning site with little effort.

- *Do not compete with billion-dollar corporations.* I have seen so many one-person Web shops kill themselves trying to design a site that's better than Yahoo or a store that's better than Amazon.com. If you had similar ambitions in mind, let me spare you the pain: don't even attempt it. These and other companies like them have hundreds of people working full time on their sites. They have state-of-the-art equipment, in-house artists, professional programmers, and steady paychecks. You have none of that going for you. Moreover, you're not even competing with them. People will never think of your site as a place to find everything they need on the Web, but they'll think of Yahoo. They will never think of your site as a place to buy almost anything, but they'll think of Amazon.com. You are not competing with billion-dollar corporations. You are competing against the collective weight of the Internet to get a tiny trickle of its traffic. That's all.

• *Do not try to create the most sophisticated site.* Here again, you will never be able to out-tech full-time Web design firms. They will always produce better components that will razzle and dazzle an audience. You're not going for that anyway. Most people have long since grown bored with another "cool" site. We've seen it already! We've seen special effects from Hollywood for years. How impressed will we be by a jumping icon? Not very, so don't waste your time or the download time of your visitors on something that's a yawn anyway. Let the expensive design firms waste their time and the download time of their clients' visitors.

• *Keep your time commitment reasonable.* Create a site that requires only a few hours of your week. That means you're not going to compete with Reuters to get fast-breaking news to the Internet. A friend of mine tried that—for about three hours. You're not going to post a digital screen saver designed by you every day. You're not going to change the colors of your site every hour on the hour.

• *Do a few things very well.* The best way to succeed as a one-person Web shop is to specialize. Create a simple, elegant design and stick with it. Then fill your site gradually with content that is uniquely yours. You don't need to rework the entire site just to keep it interesting to new visitors. In fact, few will ever move past your first page. Just change the content on the first page and archive your previous content in other sections of the site. That allows people who visit frequently to see the newest material immediately while allowing newcomers to dig deeper for some of your classic material. One of the best examples of a successful site that specializes in one thing is **www.drudgereport.com**. This is reporter Matt Drudge's site where he broke the news story about President Clinton's affair with Monica Lewinsky. Drudge posts a strange or revealing story every day or two at his site. That's all. He doesn't change the design. He doesn't provide anything more than text. He doesn't even archive old material for more than a few days. He just writes a single story, then posts it to his site. Because they are good stories and people want to know, Drudge welcomes more than one million visitors each day.

• *Offer timeless material.* To be even less involved than Matt Drudge, I suggest that you focus on material that never expires. Instead of an essay about today's top news, why not offer advice that will be just as pertinent two years from now as it is today? That's what I do at my site with financial tips, book reviews, and life observations. Very little of what I post to the Web ever loses its appeal. It does move from the top page to a lower section, however. You don't want to create what is called a *cobweb*, parlance for a site that never changes.

• *Reuse popular material.* Once you have a foundation of material that is tried-and-true, reuse it. There's nothing wrong with dropping a popular article down to a subsection of your site for several months, making it resurface on the top page for a week, then sending it back to the subsection. The best design is to never have the article change location at all. You simply add a bit of teaser text to your top page and a link to the article. It's still listed in the subsection where it permanently resides. You've just offered a front-page promotion for it. This technique allows you to get a lot of mileage out of the hard work you've done in the past and keeps your site appearing fresh. Of course you should also be developing new material to go with the re-used classic material.

## Create a Do and Don't Table

Take a sheet of paper and draw a line down the middle. Label the left-hand side "Do" and the right-hand side "Don't." Keep this paper with you at all times as you embark on your Web design journey. When a design idea strikes you, write it down immediately in the Do column. When an enormous mistake whacks you upside the head, write it down immediately in the Don't column. This two-column table will prove invaluable as you build your online business.

This section will bulk up your Do and Don't table with three activities: reading two Web design books, conducting a similar-site survey, and visiting Web design sites.

### Read Two Web Design Books

There are enough books written about Web design to cover your desk. Two shine from the shelf brighter than the rest. I suggest that you purchase both of them and keep them nearby as you create and later modify your site.

The first book is *The Non-Designer's Web Book: An Easy Guide to Creating, Designing, and Posting Your Own Web Site* by Robin Williams and John Tollett. The title says it all. You'll learn basic principles of design like alignment, repetition, and contrast. From there, the book gets specific to the Web with sections on color, graphics, typography, and tables.

The second book is the Yale University Press *Web Style Guide: Basic Design Principles for Creating Web Sites* by Peter Lynch and Sarah Horton. This is the definitive guide to creating sites based not on fashion and technology, but on long-established rules of design. It's a user-centered approach, too, which is exactly what you should have foremost in mind for attracting and keeping customers.

Remember to keep notes in your Do and Don't table as you read each book. That's where you can customize timeless design information to the site you're gradually designing in your mind. For instance, you might read a section on site navigation methods and an idea will pop into your mind. "Hey, since I'm selling pinecone wreaths, I could use pine boughs for buttons to different sections of my site. When a visitor clicks one, it will change into a finished wreath to show which section of the site they're in." Write it down in your Do column. It might not win out in the end, but it's worth experimenting.

## Conduct a Similar-Site Survey

The best way to get your creative juices flowing is to hop on the Web and visit sites that are similar to yours. It's important that they be similar. Remember that an artist should not put her portfolio on a page that was designed for a tax management seminar. That means an artist should look at art sites. A tax professional should look at tax planning sites. Decide what kind of site you're going to design, then search for others of its ilk.

When you arrive at each site, pay close attention to the following items.

- *How quickly does the site load?* This is a critical point. It doesn't matter how cool or helpful or offensive a site is if it takes so long to load that people give up and leave. They will never see it. If they never see it, they'll never come back. If they never come back, they'll never buy anything. Watch the second hand on your watch and consider how long is too long for you to wait. Most Web design professionals say that the first page should load in ten seconds or less.

- *Is there anything interesting to see during the load time?* Some sites intelligently place text elements right up front that load in an instant. The remaining graphics and tables and banners that take a bit longer gradually appear over the remainder of the load time. This is a great approach because it immediately gives the visitor something to see or do while waiting for the entire page to materialize.

- *What's your first impression of the site?* Your very first impression is the load time. But past that, what do you think of the site when it's finally staring you in the face? The first impression determines whether a visitor will explore the site. If they don't like the first page enough to see what else is available, they'll leave and probably never come back. That's bad for business.

• *Are there way too many colors or conflicting graphics?* There's a tendency to get circuslike on the Web. With a palette of colors limited only by human eyesight, people often think that the more colors they use the fancier they look. In fact, it's often just the opposite. A touch of color, a single well-placed graphic, and a dash of thematic bullets go far in creating a pleasant page with little distraction.

• *How easily can you get to the good stuff?* My personal design directive is to keep all content within three clicks. That means a visitor would arrive at my homepage, click once to go to a subsection, click again to go to an area of the subsection, and click a third time to get to a specific document. That's the maximum, mind you. It's better if they can click once and go directly to the information they need. The best situation of all is when they find what they need immediately on the first page. You visited **www.networksolutions.com** in the last section to register your domain name. Remember how the entry field to get your domain name was at the top of the very first page? That's excellent design. The company knows that everybody visiting them wants to register a name, so they made it the most obvious element at their site. No need to hunt around for a button that says "Register a Domain." It's looking right at you.

• *Can you tell what else is at the site?* There are so many homepages that provide a blast of information or cool graphics without the tiniest clue as to what else is available at the site. Visitors don't want to have to figure anything out. It takes time and it takes brain power that they'd rather devote to getting the information they want. This is especially important if a site provides practical information such as movie times, restaurant lists, weather reports, or traffic updates. A site should try to determine why people will be visiting, then put the answer to that question directly in front of them or at least make it obvious how they can get to the answers.

- *Do you like the navigation menu?* The navigation menu is the collection of buttons and links that connects you to the rest of the site. Some are along the side of the page, some are at the top, some are at the bottom, and some are scattered around. When you click from the homepage to a content page, can you still see the navigation menu or did it disappear entirely? After a few clicks, do you have any idea where you are on the site?

## Visit Web Design Sites

Now that you've got a few ideas from sites similar to the one you're planning, you should stop by some of the professional website design shops. There you'll find lots of timesaving tips and pointers to good features that you can add to your site for free. Be sure to bookmark the sites you're about to visit so you can stop back frequently in the never-ending quest to keep your site among the Web's best.

Your first stop is **www.builder.com**. Builder.com describes itself as "The Site for Site Builders." It contains essays on good page design, workshops on graphics formatting, and links to cool tools that will help your site stand out from the crowd. Builder.com has tutorials for the first-time site designer and in-depth instructions for pros.

Your second stop is **www.developer.com**. This site proclaims itself as the "Leading Source for Technical Information" and covers programming, search techniques, scripts, HTML tricks, database integration, and tools that you can download. Developer.com targets the techie audience.

Your third stop is **www.hotwired.com/webmonkey**. Webmonkey likes to toy around with sites and make them the best they can be. The site itself is an example of good contemporary design, and the content is hard to beat. With articles, graphics collections, and tutorials, Webmonkey is sure to drop something useful out of the tree.

**Good Design Will Make Your Site Shine**

Your fourth stop is **www.sitelaunch.net**. As its name implies, Sitelaunch offers everything you need to launch your site into orbit. Its style and design section will be most useful to you at this point, but later you'll want to delve into its promotion sections, cool tools list, and free site add-ons.

Your fifth stop is **webdesign.about.com**, one of the best collections of design resources available. You'll find links directly to articles at design sites, thus saving yourself the hassle of navigating the sites yourself. Like all About.com sections, this one is managed by a human being and updated regularly.

For an extra credit stop try Dmitry's Design Lab at **www.webreference.com/dlab**. Dmitry Kirsanov is a Web designer based in St. Petersburg, Russia. His monthly articles on all aspects of Web design are some of the prettiest you'll read. He views the Web as a chance for everybody to express themselves, and his love of the medium comes through in his articles.

Finally, there's a design site specifically for users of NetObjects Fusion design software at **www.efuse.com**. Although it lists design steps that everybody should follow, its examples and screen captures all come from the Fusion software. If you chose Fusion for yourself after reading about it on pages 47–48, you'll want to take a look at eFuse.

If you would like to see more resources, visit the only search engine for webmasters, BrainFind at **www.brainfind.com**. Whatever questions you have, somebody's brain holds the answers. It's just a matter of finding that brain.

## The Big Tips

Your Do and Don't table should be fairly complete by now. Between the two design books, the sites similar to yours, and the online design shops, I would expect that you know more about what constitutes a good site than the average weekend Web designer.

However, there are several biggies that I want to make sure you don't miss. Just in case they slipped through your research somehow, I will present them to you here. As you read, check to make sure you've noted the tip somewhere on your Do and Don't table. If you haven't, add it to the appropriate column.

• DO keep your site within a 640-pixel width. Doing so will ensure that people with small monitors can still see it in an attractive manner. This is especially important as Web browsing moves from computers to small portable devices. Having to scroll down is fine because people expect content to flow past the bottom of the screen. Just make sure that the most important part of each page appears within the top 460 pixels of length so it's seen by every viewer without having to scroll down. Having to scroll sideways is a big no-no. You can feel safe that anything within the 640 × 460 pixel sweet spot is viewable by nearly all computer users.

• DON'T dominate a page with decorations. People want something useful from your website, not another cute graphic or flashing lightning bolt. If a page is nothing but decorations, why is it even part of your site? The only reason I can think of is that you sell website decorations!

• DO use a navigation system that appears the same on every page. It should tell users where they are and provide quick ways to get somewhere else.

• DON'T use clumsy, oversize buttons for navigation. They take up too much space and look stupid.

• DO underline all links and choose a color that goes well with the colors used in the rest of your site. The default blue link color is not set in stone. You can make links whatever color you'd like. All three of the design programs you read about on page 47 let you set a preference for link colors across your entire site. For instance, you can elect to make all unclicked links dark purple and all clicked links light purple.

• DON'T format large blocks of text in bold, italics, or all caps. Also, don't underline anything that is not a link. It makes your site confusing. People on the Web expect underlined text to link them to additional information.

• DO use graphics sparingly. They should break up long blocks of text and should preferably be small. That's it.

Don't show pretty mountain landscapes or ocean vistas unless they pertain to what your site is all about.

• DON'T make anything blink or move. This is a safe path to take. Blinking and animation are instantly confusing and unprofessional. Even if an animation is cute or funny, people tire of it after the first two or three seconds. If you must include an animation, use one that moves very slowly or stops moving after a couple seconds. The worst animations jump all over the page and make noises. I visited one site that was so bad I began flogging my screen with a fly swatter.

• DO use an alt label on every graphic. An alt label is a line of text that appears when a graphic doesn't load properly and when the user hovers the cursor above the graphic. There are people who view the Web through nongraphical browsers. The alt label gives them something to understand what is supposed to be pictured at your site. Your website design program allows you to easily add alt labels to every graphic.

• DON'T litter your site with garbage. Garbage is anything that distracts from your main focus for no reason. It doesn't benefit you or the visitor, yet some sites still keep garbage in plain view. Hit counters are garbage. Nobody cares how many other people have visited your site. If you care, monitor the figure somewhere besides your site. Don't waste valuable screen space. Any page that is under construction is garbage. Nobody wants to know what is coming soon from your website. They only want to see what is there and working now. Never keep pages that are under construction plastered with the yellow "under construction" icon of men at work. Buttons from Microsoft that point people to the Internet Explorer site and from AOL/Netscape that point people to the Navigator site are garbage. Everybody already has the software or is aware of it. They don't need to see it advertised on your site to learn about the browsers. Worst of all, you are sacrificing valuable space and download time to provide billion-dollar companies with free advertising that in no way benefits you or your site. "Wow! Check this out, honey. Microsoft has a Web browser that we can download for free. I discovered it right here at Lazy Jane's website. I'm going to tell everybody about this valuable tip from Lazy Jane so they will all visit her site!" Nobody will ever say that, so leave the ad graphics off.

• DO use transparent graphics. Some graphics have a colored background and a border around them. They look much better if the color and border disappear so that the main graphic stands by itself against the site background. This is called transparency. While almost all good graphics packages use transparent graphics, there are still some that do not. Be sure that you choose only the ones that are transparent or you use a graphics program to make your graphics transparent. It may seem like a small detail, but it's not. A site that is sprinkled with graphics surrounded by squares of entirely mismatched colors can cause epileptic seizures.

## Sketch Your Site

Before you begin typing or clicking in your design software, sketch out your site on a piece of paper. Sketching is easier for your mind to handle. You've been doing it since you were a kid, so there's nothing confining about it. In your design software, no matter how well you know it, there's always a certain way you're forced to get things done. That makes creativity difficult. So walk away from the computer with your extensive list of do's and don'ts from your site survey, and sketch the way you want your site to appear.

You should actually make several sketches. The first one should be an outline of your site so you know what goes where. This will also help you come up with a design for each page based on how many sections you need to help the user navigate. For instance, if you have five hundred pages at your site, your navigation system is going to be far more complicated than if you have just five pages.

In sketching your site outline, you can do it either hierarchically like an org chart or in traditional outline form. Here's a simple outline of my initial five-page site in org chart form:

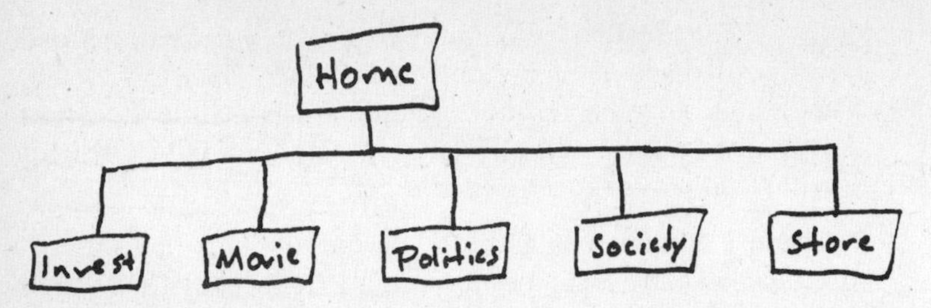


You can decide for yourself which method is easiest for you to use. For me, the hierarchical method is a better way to plan a website because I think of exploring a site as digging deep into it. The top-down scheme looks more like something I would dig into as opposed to something I would dig sideways. Your design software will allow you to arrange pages in either fashion.

When you have an idea for what sections and subsections you want at your site, you should sketch your homepage design. Place the banner, the navigation menu, text blocks, pictures, and other major elements that you've decided should be part of your site. Keep experimenting until you get something that looks like what you had in mind.

Also, try new arrangements. Most sites place the navigation buttons on the left side of the pages and a banner along the top. Perhaps you'd like your buttons along the top as well or even along the right side of the page. Maybe you have something entirely new in mind. There's nothing to lose by playing with the design on paper.

Here's what the initial design sketch of my homepage looked like:

Text Button
Text Button
Jason Kelly
Text Button
Text Button
TEXT
TEXT
Small Banner Ad
TEXT
TEXT
Investments | Movies
Politics | Society | Store
B
O
O
K
S
$ $ $ $ $
Feature
TEXT
Kelly's Quicklist

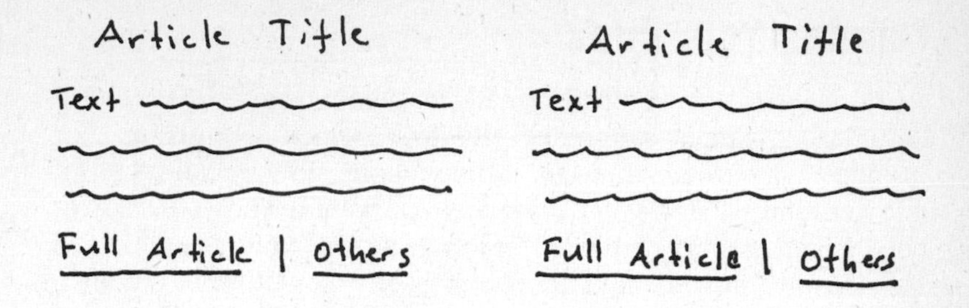


Visit **www.jasonkelly.com** and notice that it didn't turn out exactly this way. When you translate your sketch onto the computer screen, things change. A certain font looks better and changes the size of your main menu. A picture looks awkward so you drop it. The transition from paper to screen is an evolutionary one where creativity meets practicality.

But don't worry about that when you're sketching your initial design. Just let your dream site flow from your fingertips down the pencil to the paper.

# Building Your Site

After you've toyed with a number of design ideas and have a good notion what your site should look like, it's time to build it. The mechanics of this part are simple. You sit at your computer and fire up your Web design software. You go to the site management section and lay out the site in the same org chart or outline fashion that you sketched. Then, you open the homepage and begin creating the elements that will make up each page. Your site will need a title banner, navigation menu, text, graphics, and everything else that you sketched.

This section shows how to name your files, where to find free graphics, some excellent features that anybody can use on their site for free, and a quick way to fine-tune your site.

## Naming Your Files

As a website grows from small to medium to large, poorly thought-out names can make site management confusing. For instance, say you write an article about flowers and call it "flower.html." Later, you decide that you want to showcase flower books in an entirely dedicated flower section of your site. You call the section "flower" and the book page "flower.html." Wait a minute, says your design program, you already have a file called "flower.html." No problem, you reply, and specify that the book page should be "flower2.html." Later, you add to the flower section of your site, and every new file is numerically incremented so that you have "flower3.html," "flower4.html," and so on.

Pretty soon, you don't know which flowerX.html file is which. One of them is an article, one is a photo gallery, one is a bookstore, one is another article. Ugh. Now you've got to visit each flower file individually to remember which one is which so that you are sure to link to the right one.

**Name Your Files Carefully**

To avoid this situation, decide on a naming convention. A naming convention is a set of rules you use to name files consistently for easy management. In this case, you could help yourself by preceding the word *flower* with the type of page. Perhaps an article would be preceded by "art," a picture gallery by "pic," and a commercial store by "com." Now you at least have subdivisions within all the flower files: artflower1.html, artflower2.html, picflower1.html, comflower1.html, and so on.

That's a good approach, but could be improved even more. If the day ever comes when you've generated ten or more files of the same flower type, your files will no longer be sorted in order. Why? Because the computer thinks that "artflower2" should come after "artflower10." To avoid this, simply use a zero in front of the single-digit numbers. Thus, "artflower01.html," "art flower02.html," all the way until you reach "artflower10.html." Of course, this will only work until you reach "artflower100.html," but do you really think you'll write 100 articles about flowers? For most people, the answer is probably no. If you are running a flower site, the answer might be yes. In that case, simply add two zeros to get "artflower001.html" and so on. That'll get you up to 999 flower articles all sorted properly from first to last.

Now, it may occur to you that if you have 999 flower articles, your naming convention isn't going to be very helpful in finding the right one anymore. That's true, but with 999 files of any type you will not be able to capture all the identifying information in the file name alone. To help yourself, I suggest a file table with three columns. Put the file name in the left column, the date of creation in the middle column, and a description of the file's contents in the right column. This way, you can glance at the file table to see which file is which. You can keep the table in a word-processing file on your computer for quick updates as you add and remove files from your site.

If you are generating a huge volume of files, consider using a date naming convention. If you write a new article on November 21, 2000, you would title it 20001121.html. This is just the year (2000), the month (11), and the day (21). If you wrote two articles that day, you would use alphabetical designations after the date. In this case, 20001121a.html and 20001121b.html.

With a date naming convention, you know nothing about the article except the day it was written and posted to your site. The advantages to date naming are that your files are always properly sorted and new files are automatically named, with no effort needed to dream up a good name. Combined with a file table, date naming can be a great way to manage large sites.

Use your own preference in choosing a naming convention, but do yourself a favor and decide on one from the first day you build your site. It's a hassle to make changes later, and it's confusing to decide on a naming convention that only applies to files created after a certain date.

## Where to Find Free Graphics

While you don't want to clutter your site with too many graphics or dog your visitors with large graphics that take forever to load, you do want to use small graphics artistically to break up long blocks of text and create a pleasant look. You can buy CDs full of Web-ready graphics at any software store. However, there are lots of free graphics just waiting for you on the Internet.

You may be surprised to learn that any graphic you see anywhere on the Web is yours for the taking. All you do is right-click your mouse on it and select the "Save Picture As . . ." command to put it right on your hard drive. You can use it in word processing documents, spreadsheets, and your website. It's not always legal to take somebody's copyrighted graphic, but often they won't mind. That's especially true if you provide a reciprocal link back to their website for the privilege of being able to use their graphic. If you have questions, e-mail the site administrator and ask. I've never been denied the use of a graphic or even some text once I asked politely and promised a reciprocal link.

That's an important technique to remember. Few graphic sites will have the quality or a collection of images specific to your topic area that a topical site will have. For example, a SCUBA diving site is going to use much better underwater graphics than you'll ever find at a general graphics site. An investment site will use much better business icons than you'll find at a general graphics site. So your first search for great graphics should always be among sites that have similar topics to the one you're working on.

The general graphics sites are, for the most part, not worth your time. They're clumsily put together, parade dozens of blinking buttons past your eyes, and only serve up a handful of dull graphics for your trouble. Even if you find something you like, chances are that others have found it and have used it on so many sites that people go into a near coma every time they see it appear again on their screen.

The rainbow divider line is a perfect example. A few years ago it became the coolest thing to show on your website. Then, to make it really cool, people began running a spark along it. Because rainbows have so many colors, the divider line never matches the sites where it appears. It's completely generic, which is why you'll find the rainbow divider at so many general graphics sites and why you should run screaming in the opposite direction every time it's offered to you.

If you decide that you must browse the free balls, bullets, buttons, and rainbow divider lines available on the Web, then stop by **www.aaaclipart.com** and **www.arttoday.com**. To scrounge around a few more sites, check out the listings at **www.clipart.com** and **www.reallybig.com/clipart.shtml**.

## Excellent Free Features

How would you like to add a search box to your website that allows people to find information from related sites? Perhaps you want to survey your visitors to discover what they like and dislike about your site. These two features and lots of others are available to you for free.

Sites like to develop features and give them away because doing so creates pointers all over the Web back to the originating site. For instance, when somebody uses a HotBot search box, they find results at HotBot's page. When people view customized news headlines through the Yahoo To Go feature, they do so at Yahoo's news site. More free features on more sites means more traffic. Traffic means money, and that's what everybody wants.

Some of the search engines offer a way for you to offer a customizable search box to your page. For the most part, I find this useless because nobody is going to think to visit your site for searching the Internet. However, you can restrict these search functions to sites that maintain a certain focus. For instance, if you are building an automotive site, it would be helpful to your visitors to offer a search box that looks only at automotive sites. You can also add a feature that allows visitors to search your site for specific information. That becomes especially helpful as your site grows.

The customizable search engines I like best are from HotBot tools at **www.hotbot.com/help/tools**, SmartLinks at **www.looksmart.com/smartlinks**, whatUseek at **www.whatuseek.com/webmaster**, and Yahoo To Go at **docs.yahoo.com/docs/yahootogo**. Both HotBot and SmartLinks allow you to specify which sites you want the search box to focus on and place such predefined searches into a pull-down list. The SmartLinks box even includes icons that point people to news and weather pages. Also, SmartLinks offers you a choice of receiving free banner advertising or payment for traffic that you direct to its site through your search box. The whatUseek search feature provides a number of customizations for making the results page look like your own website. Yahoo To Go isn't as full-featured as the other three but does include a nifty news search function that lets you create a predefined headline search. Thus, you could create a button to the latest news about automobile racing, adoption in America, or the search for extraterrestrial intelligence.

The list of free features on the Web is almost endless. Want to add a daily trivia game to your site? It's available at **www.uproar.com/webdevelopers/intro.html**. How about special effects with dynamic HTML? They are all for free at **www.dynamicdrive.com**. Perhaps you'd like to poll your site visitors with the simple tools at **www.pollit.com**.

**They've Got All the Features You Need**

The biggest collection of miscellaneous features that I know of is Looksmart's Beseen service at **www.beseen.com**. You'll begin to wonder why anybody spends time building their own sites after viewing all you can get for free. As I write this, Beseen offers search tools, a survey program called Quizlet, a chat room, a bulletin board, a hit counter, an ad banner exchange, Web-based e-mail that displays your site logo, a guest book, and a navigation robot. All of this is supposed to make your site more appealing so that it will "be seen." Get it?

Now, just because all of this stuff is yours for the taking does not necessarily mean that you need to take all of it. Be discerning. Only choose what will truly add something of value to your website. A page full of completely unrelated capabilities won't impress anybody past an initial "Hmm, that's sort of cool."

You want lasting appeal. Treat these features like makeup: They can accentuate an already great site, but they can't turn a terrible site into something wonderful. Your unique content and design should be your main attractions.

## Fine-tuning Your Site

When you've got your site designed and built and sprinkled with appropriate features, take a moment now and then to fine-tune it. You want fast-loading graphics, pages that look good in every browser, and links that actually work.

These quick checks and more are available for free on the Internet. For a small fee, you can subscribe to services that will send an automated robot to your site every week to check all the plumbing and provide you with a complete report. That's probably overkill, but it's there if you want it.

You fine-tune your car in a car garage, so it makes sense to fine-tune your website in the website garage. You'll find it at **www.websitegarage.com**, where you supply your site address and e-mail address for a free monthly tune-up and newsletter. Take a look at the GIF Lube tool that will crawl through your site and compress all the graphics once per month. It costs $10 per site.

For a completely free tune-up, skip the garage and go straight to the mechanic. NetMechanic, that is, found at **www.netmechanic.com**. All the usual link checking, code checking, browser checking, and load-time checking tools are there, plus the best free graphics reduction program on the Internet. It's called GIFBot. You tell it your site address and click the OPTIMIZE button. It processes your top page and returns a list of all the graphics and their sizes. Click on a graphic's file size for a selection of the same image at varying degrees of reduction such as 20 percent, 30 percent, 50 percent, 80 percent, and 90 percent. You will instantly see which version best balances file size with image quality and can then save that version to your hard drive. On your website, replace bloated images with smaller ones for great-looking pages that download in half the time. Not bad for a free utility, eh?

## Creating Content for Your Site

There's a saying in the Web industry that "content is king." It means that for all the killer technology, pretty graphics, and interactive programming available on the Web, what people really want is valuable information. If you provide it, nobody will care that it's on a stripped-down website or even in plain text. Many Web users would actually prefer that it be presented that way.

Not every site defines content in the same way. On my site and lots of other small sites, content means articles. They're easy to create, easy to prepare for online viewing, and they load quickly. Text is the most basic way of communicating online.

Some sites define content as updated factual information like stock market performance, weather reports, government grants that just became available, or concert schedules. Still other sites define content as their well-stocked online store with a few niceties thrown in for kicks. Amazon.com, for example, has more content than almost any other site. Most of it is contained in the 4.5 million book listings that are filled with reader comments and professional reviews. People go to the site to read about books that interest them, and then they buy those books. Even at this overtly commercial site, content plays a vital role.

It plays a vital role at your site too. Presumably, you decided to create a website with some idea of what you'd put on it. You probably thought that your interests translated into an online destination would be useful to people and could even make you some extra money.

Only you can know for certain how best to present your interests online. No matter what you decide on, however, I suggest that you include articles. They lend themselves to every profession and hobby on the planet. They are the ultimate example of people getting help online. I can't count the number of times I've heard somebody say, "I saw this on the Internet" or "I printed out a great article about that from the Web."

Either write articles yourself or find somebody to write them for you. Make them timeless so that people will find them helpful and then point their friends to your site to read the articles. Some items that I wrote three years ago still get heavy traffic today—and that's a common story online. A document called "Do All the Big Ones" at **www.virtualpromote.com** lists the Web's biggest search engines so that new website owners can get listed at all the important places. It's updated from time to time, but has been roughly the same for years. It's a legend among promoters, and almost everybody knows that the most basic step to getting seen online is to read this document at VirtualPROMOTE and then follow its leads.

Can you carve out a similarly valuable space in your field? Of course. Ask yourself what anybody entering your field absolutely needs to know. Once you have it in mind, write an article that teaches everything they need to know.

For instance, if you're building a site on butterfly collecting, you might determine that all new collectors need to know about Monarch butterflies. It's a familiar variety, and everybody should start with it. So you gather a few books at the library, your own field notes, and some magazine articles about Monarchs and type up the definitive document, "The Making of a Monarch Collector," complete with photos, scientific facts, and personal observations. If you also sell butterfly products, you can certainly list them at appropriate places in the article, and it might be a good idea to provide a bibliography of the books you used in writing the article—for sale through your affiliate account at Amazon.com, of course. More on that in Chapter 5.

**The Ultimate Butterfly Site, Butterfly Included**

If you don't enjoy writing or don't have time, consider hiring others in your field to write articles for you. You will find that many people are eager to express themselves in a public forum, and a large percentage of ordinary folks are good at doing it. Payment arrangements vary. I know friends who sell their articles outright for anywhere from $20 to $5,000. I know others who write simply to get the *byline*—that's their name listed as the author.

A third arrangement that seems to work well online is a sales commission. If somebody writes an article for your site that becomes the main reason people visit, you could share a portion of your site's revenue with that author. A better way to approach this is to track the sales volume that originates from an author's articles. That way, you're not sharing too much of your revenue and the author is paid by the quality and appeal of her work. When I first began running articles by a friend of mine, I sold related products from his pages and tracked the sales of those products. When I received my quarterly checks for items sold, it was a simple matter to calculate what percentage of the money should go to my friend.

If you want to get truly serious about the content at your website, consider paying a syndication service. You can receive a list of headlines that are updated periodically or, for more money, complete stories.

To learn more, look at **www.isyndicate.com**. The company's Express program is a free way to provide your visitors with world news headlines, daily horoscopes, and similar general interest material. I'm not sure this content adds a whole lot of value to your site because it isn't specific to your niche and people can find it almost anywhere. World news at your site? Come on. People will get that from CNN or ABC or MSNBC or even, I dare say, newspapers. Still, if you want to bulk up your site for free, the content is available.

The iSyndicate Network is a whole different breed of cat. Starting at $500 per month, Network accounts have access to thousands of full-length articles. iSyndicate will even marry the material to your niche and automatically update it with fresh content. Network members could build an entire site around syndicated content without ever typing a single paragraph on their own.

iSyndicate is not alone. The *Los Angeles Times*'s new media division syndicates features at **www.timeslink.com**. Some of the more popular features are "World's Fare" for travel sites, a golf course guide with a database of more than 17,500 courses, John Gray's "Men Are from Mars, Women Are from Venus" advice column, and Sydney Omarr's astrological forecasts. Pricing is based on how much content you use.

Not to be outdone, the *New York Times* syndicate offers specialized content for websites at **www.nytsyn.com/online**. You can get computer news from Computer News Daily, health news from Your Health Daily, entertainment news from Entertainment News Daily, and so on.

Unless you see your site becoming one of the Web's main hubs and you expect to draw enormous amounts of traffic, syndication services are probably unnecessary. Nobody will come to love your site because it carries today's horoscope, which they also read in the newspaper and saw on the morning television programs. They will come to love your site because it offers them unique information that would not be available to them if not for the amazing technology of the Internet.

Specialized information is what gives little sites a fighting chance. Whatever method of creating content you choose, make sure that your visitors know they've come to a gem of a site that specializes in something.

## Tracking Your Site

You know that the name of the game in a Web business is traffic. The volume of people visiting your site on a regular basis will determine how much income your site generates. This is a simple concept to understand because it works the same way in a traditional store with a roof and four walls.

The difference is that you know how many people come into your traditional store by watching them. When Mr. Smith opens the door, you hear bells ring perhaps and you see Mr. Smith's body moving from one product display to the next. Your eyes tell your brain, "We have a customer in the store." You may even interact with Mr. Smith by saying—not typing—hello.

On your website, you can't see Mr. Smith walk in the front door. He might come in through your homepage, click to several of your articles, browse your store, bookmark your site for another visit later, then leave. None of which is apparent to you unless your site is tracked.

Tracking your site means monitoring the level of traffic, the origins of that traffic, and the behavior of that traffic within your site. It's all very useful in helping you devise a marketing strategy.

As with most other online tools, you can find free tracking services on the Internet. Also, your hosting company probably provides basic traffic statistics through your control panel, which is paid for by your monthly hosting fee.

I have found, however, that the comprehensive tracking that

can be yours for free or less than $10 per month is usually better than that provided by your hosting package. It is customizable, so you can examine patterns from the past day, week, month, or year. One small insight gained from watching such patterns can increase your traffic and income.

**Track Your Site Thoroughly**

SiteTracker at **www.sitetracker.com** shows an hourly traffic graph, which search engines your visitors used, which search terms your visitors found you with, what browsers your visitors run, which Web pages visitors came to your site from, the average load time of your site at different times of day, and a truckload of other statistics. The service offers two ways for you to pay. The first option is for you to display banner ads on behalf of SiteTracker's advertisers. The second is for you to pay $6 per month with no obligation to display banners. Because you will have no control over who is advertising on your site and almost all free online banners are tacky looking and a waste of space, I suggest that paying the $6 per month is a better choice. To compare a nearly identical service, take a quick look at **www.superstats.com**.

If you don't mind displaying a banner ad or button on your site, then try the service at **www.hitbox.com**. The banners and buttons point your visitors to the HitBox search engine, which uses statistics from the HitBox tracking program to rank sites. So this is actually a multipurpose tool. It provides you with thorough site tracking and also gets your site listed in a search engine. The service is free, but you must display the company's graphic at your site. If you don't, then the tracking software won't work. To see a compilation of statistics from all sites using the HitBox tracker, visit **www.statmarket.com**.

No matter how you decide to track your website, remember to keep the number of visitors to yourself. As you were advised in the design section of this chapter, don't put one of those silly hit counters on your site. You might be tempted to do so because you think that displaying the number of past visitors will convince newcomers of your site's merit.

Wrong. There are only two amounts that your hit counter

can display: few hits or many hits. In the case of few hits, your first-time visitors are going to see the small number and decide that the site is probably not worth their while. The low-hit counter will discourage them from exploring your site. In the case of many hits, your site is already popular because of something you're doing. You have good content, a fresh design, or something else that people like. I guarantee that they aren't returning to your site to see how many other people have been there in the past few days. As you can see, a hit counter serves to discourage people or has no effect on them whatsoever.

Never show a hit counter on your site. Track to your heart's content, but keep the results to yourself.

# 5 Becoming an Online Affiliate

The easiest way to make immediate money off your new website is through online affiliate programs, sometimes called associate programs or partner programs. They enable you to sell products from other companies at your site and receive a commission. You don't need to take orders, collect payment, manage inventory, ship products, or provide customer service. All you do is find products that are appropriate to the content of your website, link to them, and collect a commission when they sell. It's simple and it works.

## Advantages of an Online Affiliate Site

There are four advantages to maintaining an affiliate website. They are so compelling that anybody with a website should participate.

### It Runs Twenty-four Hours a Day

While you go to work, play in the backyard, or sleep, your website is up and running. If you are an online affiliate with one or more merchants, the products you select to display for sale on your website can be purchased twenty-four hours a day. That means you can be making money all the time no matter what you're doing.

I know of few other businesses that offer that potential. Most require you to somehow participate in order for the business to operate. Even if you aren't participating directly, you need to hire others to manage the business for you.

Not with an affiliate website. The host computer does all the work in displaying your pages, while the affiliate merchant does all the work in fulfilling orders. You just design and maintain the site at your convenience, then receive checks in your mailbox on a monthly or quarterly schedule.

## It Reaches a Worldwide Audience

Remember that it's called the World Wide Web because it reaches around the world. Whether you live in the heart of New York City or on a mountaintop in Montana, you will reach the same global audience with your website affiliate store. Few other businesses offer such flexibility in location.

I've received e-mail from people who visit my site from Japan, China, Canada, Brazil, the Philippines, Australia, France, and Germany. Some of them purchased books that I offer at my site in affiliation with Amazon.com, and I receive a commission on every one of those sales. You'll experience the same diverse customer base.

Built into a large enough business, this global reach can help insulate you from local economic trouble. For example, if your community suffers a recession and you lose your job or see your business income drop, people living in more affluent communities can still visit your website and purchase items there. The Web allows money to be transferred quickly around the planet.

## It Requires No Paperwork

This is no small claim. Anybody who has ever run a traditional business knows how much paperwork is involved. There are orders to be written, inventory sheets to be filled out, and permits to be filed with the county.

As an online affiliate, you never deal with any of it. When a visitor clicks on a product that you offer, they instantly leave your website to complete their order at the merchant's website. At that point, it's out of your hands. The merchant takes care of all details including a commission credit to your account.

The only piece of paper you'll ever see is a check made payable to you. That's paperwork you probably won't mind handling!

## It Entails No Risk

Traditional business is risky. It requires a lot of money to be spent on something that you hope will work. If it does, you recoup your initial investment and make more money. If it doesn't, you lose your investment.

Plus, it's a big task to manage a traditional business, where you shoulder all the financial obligations. You need to track customers, orders, inventory, and bank account balances in an intricate pattern of dependencies. You can't fulfill the order until you have inventory. You can't buy inventory until you have money in the bank. You won't have money in the bank until you fulfill orders. Unless you figure this chicken-and-egg situation out soon, you won't have any customers. A business without customers can't survive for long.

Online affiliate programs eliminate all this risk because they don't cost a penny. The worst-case scenario is that you spend time finding products that will appeal to your visitors and then fail to sell any of them. You lose only your time. Your money is still safe in the bank.

This last advantage is what makes online affiliate programs such an easy choice. Because there is no risk in trying them, everybody should do it.

# How Much You Can Earn

You probably won't quit your day job after registering with affiliate merchants, but you might be able to afford a car payment or reduce your credit card balance to zero. One thing is certain, however. Affiliate sales are a big part of online commerce. According to Internet consulting firm Jupiter Communications, affiliate sales account for as much as one quarter of all online spending.

There are three variables in determining the amount of money you'll make from affiliate programs. They are the products you sell, how successfully you sell them, and how much traffic your site gets.

- *The products you sell.* Most affiliate programs pay you a sales commission of between 5 and 25 percent. The commission often varies based on the particular product you offer. Sometimes hot products that sell at a cheap price will pay you a lower commission than less popular products selling at higher prices. It all comes down to the profit margins of the merchant. If there's more money to go around, they're usually willing to share more of it with you. You will make different rates of commission on different products—even if they come from the same merchant.

- *How successfully you sell them.* The next variable is the volume of product that you sell. Obviously, a site that sells one hundred items for $50 each will make more than a site that sells only thirty of those same items. Your ability to sell products to the people who visit your site depends on how well you design your site. There's a proper balance between being effective and being appealing that you will learn about later in this chapter.

- *How much traffic your site gets.* The final variable is how much traffic your site gets. Let's say your sales rate to visitors is 10 percent. That is, one out of ten visitors buys something from you. If you have ten people visit your site, you'll sell one product. If you have ten thousand people visit your site, you'll sell one thousand products. Your ability to attract traffic to your site depends on the quality of its content, its design, and your marketing strategy. You read about content and design in Chapter 4. You'll read about marketing in Chapter 6.

## When You Are Paid

Most affiliate programs pay on a monthly schedule. They tally all the sales you made during a month and mail a check to you for the amount due. Other programs do so on a quarterly basis.

But to keep costs low, most affiliate programs hold your payment until the amount due reaches a minimum level, say $10. That way, they aren't mailing checks for 50 cents every month.

Some site owners I've spoken with have run into trouble by joining too many affiliate programs and spreading their sales too thin. They have a high enough volume to make a decent amount of money, but the volume is being divided across dozens of affiliate merchants, so the amount earned at any single one isn't enough to get paid regularly.

For instance, if you sell 100 items per month at a commission of $2 each, your site is earning $200 a month. If all that business is directed at a single merchant then you'll be paid regularly. However, if the 100 items are sold by 50 different merchants, you'll only be averaging $4 per month from each merchant. Your overall earnings are the same, but because the amount is divided across so many different affiliates you will not be paid regularly.

This is an extreme example, but makes a good point: It's better to maximize your sales at a handful of good affiliate programs than it is to join every one under the sun. The minimum payment factor is one key reason. The other key reason is that using too many merchants will make it difficult for you to target your audience.

## What Programs Are Available

There are affiliate programs for everything. The first successful affiliate program was created by Amazon.com to sell books. With more than 260,000 members, it is still the leader. But there's plenty more to sell than books, music, and videos. There are affiliate programs to sell art, toys, vacations, investments, and even real estate. In this section, I'll present the leaders in each major category and the affiliate directories where you can browse thousands of programs.

## The Leaders

There are high-quality, reliable affiliate programs and there are shady programs. I have collected a sampling of the high-quality ones I know you can trust. In addition to being honest, they offer products that just about any site can sell and lucrative commission schedules. Start by looking closely at these merchants and registering with the ones appropriate for your site.

- **Amazon.com** Here's the company that started it all. Amazon.com continues adding new products to its store, most of which you can sell from your site and earn a commission. There are free electronic greeting cards, online auctions, and more than 4.7 million books, CDs, videos, DVDs, and computer games. Amazon.com stands out from the e-commerce crowd by offering personalized recommendations, streamlined ordering through its 1-Click technology, and hassle-free auction bidding with Bid-Click. In short, Amazon.com has products that fit with any website. It should be the first affiliate program you join. You will earn 15 percent on books that you directly link and 5 percent on books that people purchase after going to the Amazon.com site from yours. You also earn 5 percent on music and videos. Checks are mailed quarterly once your commissions exceed $10.
  **www.amazon.com/associates**

- **Anaconda** This is not an affiliate program, but an enhancement to affiliate programs. The original Anaconda product was built to help Amazon.com associates earn more money by converting any book purchase from a 5 percent sale to a 15 percent sale. The product has since been expanded to cover eToys and barnesandnoble.com. Also, Anaconda offers other products that will display Amazon.com pages right on your site, update the Amazon.com Hot 100 list also on your site, and all the while make sure that every purchase qualifies for the full 15 percent commission. The products cost between $15 and $50, but pay for themselves quickly just by tripling the average commission you earn.

**www.anaconda.net**

• **Art.com** If you want to sell artwork, this is the place. Art.com keeps their beautiful site stocked with art from around the world. You will earn 15 percent commission on all sales. Checks are mailed monthly once your commissions exceed $50.

**www.art.com/affiliates**

• **Autoweb.com** People come to Autoweb.com to buy and sell automobiles. For every private owner ad placed from your website, you earn $5. For every person who requests a free price quote, you earn $2. Checks are mailed monthly once your commissions exceed $30.

**www.autoweb.com/affiliate**

• **Bach Systems** If you plan to do any advertising on your site, check out Bach Systems. It matches websites like yours with advertising clients who offer free promotions like a trial subscription to *U.S. News & World Report*, additional product information, catalogs, and sweepstakes entries. You simply use banner ads, text links, or an e-mail list to display the offers. This type of program where people do not need to actually buy anything is called pay-per-lead. You are generating sales leads, not sales. Pay-per-lead programs usually have a higher success ratio because your visitors do not spend money. At Bach Systems, you earn between 50 cents and $15 per lead, but most commissions will be less than $2. You also earn 10 percent of the revenue generated by new affiliates that you refer to Bach. Checks are mailed monthly once your commissions exceed $50. Because of a sixty-day waiting period during which Bach collects payment from clients, your monthly check usually covers the period two months prior. For example, your July check would be for May sales.

**www.bachsys.com**

• **Beyond.com** Because the Internet is a computerized medium, it makes sense to sell software. That's where Beyond.com enters the picture. Billing itself as the software superstore, it sells every kind of software imaginable. It is particularly appealing for people to buy software this way because much of it is available via Electronic Software Delivery (ESD) for instant gratification. You earn 5 percent on all shipped products and 10 percent on products delivered by ESD. Checks are mailed quarterly once your commissions exceed $75.

**www.beyond.com/affiliates/index.htm**

• **eToys** Gifts are a common item to purchase on the Web, and toys are purchased for every child's birthday. eToys is the largest toy seller online. These products might be perfect for your site if you have any content related to parenting or reviews of movies with related toys, such as *Star Wars* or the latest Disney cartoon. You earn $5 for each new customer you send to eToys and up to 12.5 percent commission. Checks are mailed quarterly once your commissions exceed $20.

**www.etoys.com/cgi-bin/affiliate form.cgi**

• **Fogdog Sports** For sports lovers, it's hard to ever leave the Fogdog site. It is to sporting goods what Amazon.com is to books. You'll find everything at cheap prices: balls, bats, and bags; clubs, caps, and crampons. You earn 10 percent on sales up to $5,000 per quarter, 15 percent on sales above $5,000 per quarter, and 20 percent on sales above $25,000 per quarter. Checks are mailed quarterly with no minimum commission requirement.

**www.fogdog.com/affiliates**

• **GiftTree** Continuing the gift theme, here's a site that offers products to give to colleagues, spouses, and neighbors. You can offer your visitors flowers, fruit baskets, bathing products, and candy arrangements. You earn 20 percent on all sales. The program is administered by Commission Junction, an affiliate management company that handles dozens of merchants. Once you register with

Commission Junction, you can join the GiftTree program as well as all others offered by Commission Junction. Checks are mailed monthly once your commissions exceed $25 for all programs that you join.
www.cj.com

• **iCreditReport.com** Like the site says, "Banks rate it, landlords screen it, employers investigate it, thieves want it, everybody wonders about it!" It's talking about credit reports. For any of your visitors who are curious to see theirs, iCreditReport.com will serve it up immediately online for $8. More thorough reports are available for $50. You earn 10 percent on all sales. Checks are mailed quarterly once your commissions exceed $50.
www.icreditreport.com/affiliate/affiliate.htm

• **JFAX** For business sites, this program is hard to pass up. JFAX products enable customers to send and receive faxes by e-mail; consolidate e-mail, faxes, and voicemail into a single messaging account; listen and respond to e-mail by Touch-Tone phone; and receive voicemail via e-mail. For traveling business people, this expanded communication power can save a lot of time. You earn 100 percent on standard sign-ups, which are usually $15. After that, you earn 5 percent on all monthly and usage fees for as long as the customer stays with JFAX. Monthly fees are usually $12.50 and certain services cost extra. Your 5 percent on the base monthly fee is 63 cents. Refer 100 people and you'll make $63 per month residual income. JFAX requires that customers keep their accounts active for at least sixty days before paying commissions. Checks are mailed quarterly once your commissions exceed $100.
webtrans.jfax.com/affiliates

• **LendingTree** The Internet has made applying for a loan simple and fast. One of the leading online loan centers is LendingTree. The company matches borrowers and lenders, saving both lots of searching. To get a loan, customers fill out one form and hear back from multiple lenders. After comparing rates and other terms, borrowers choose the best deal. LendingTree's slogan is "Apply in minutes, know within hours." They call their affiliate program the branch network. You earn $12 for each customer who goes to LendingTree, enters a valid social security number, and completes the first five pages of any qualification form. Checks are mailed monthly once your commissions exceed $30.

**www.lendingtree.com**

Sell Magazines at Your Site

• **Magazines.com** Everybody reads magazines because there's one for every interest under the sun. No matter what type of content your site provides, there's sure to be a tie-in with a subscription magazine. Magazines.com carries more than 1,200 titles at the lowest permissible prices. If you join their affiliate program, you are not allowed to offer magazines from other online magazine merchants. Of course, because Magazines.com pays the highest commissions, you wouldn't want to. You earn 25 percent on all sales. Checks are mailed quarterly once your commissions exceed $50.

**www.magazines.com**

• **MotherNature.com** Vitamins are an ever-popular health care product. If you ever write an article about health or start a section of your site devoted to it, wouldn't it be nice to include a link to related vitamins? Sure it would, and you can with MotherNature.com. The company sells more than 30,000 vitamins, minerals, and other supplements at the lowest available prices. The site also offers extensive health information and even some advice. MotherNature.com's affiliate program is administered by BeFree, one of the leading affiliate management companies. BeFree is similar to Commission Junction, which you read about in the GiftTree listing. You earn 12 percent on all sales. Checks are mailed quarterly once your commissions exceed $50.

**www.mothernature.com/affiliate/default.asp**

• **NextCard** Every site you've read about allows people to buy products or services. What do they buy with? A credit

card, of course, and NextCard offers a Visa designed for Internet consumers. It works in the real world, too, but comes with special features like online account management and a place where customers can upload a scanned photo of themselves to be printed on their card. New accounts are approved at the NextCard website in thirty seconds. Naturally, this program will work best for your site if it attracts people from higher income brackets who are interested in purchasing items online and will qualify for a credit card. You earn $20 for every new card approved. Checks are mailed monthly once your commissions exceed $50.
**banners.nextcard.com/affiliates/affiliates.shtml**

• **One & Only** Perhaps you want to spread a little love around the Web with this online service that provides matchmaking and romance personals. An advantage to this program is that it provides you with free content for your site in addition to an income opportunity. Of course, romantic content might not fit your site's theme. But if it does or you can figure a way to make it fit, the benefit of having One & Only design a customized version of its material for you—then host and maintain it for free—is too good to pass up. Topic areas that attract a large number of single people include cultural, entertainment, shopping, and travel. You earn 15 percent on each new and renewal membership. The renewal commission applies for life regardless of whether the customers ever visit your site again. Also, you earn 33 percent commissions on revenue generated by sites that you refer to the One & Only affiliate program. According to the site's own disclosure, the top individual affiliate for a recent one-year period was a fellow in New Jersey who earned $11,267. Checks are mailed monthly with no minimum commission requirement.
**www.oneandonlynetwork.com**

**And They Lived Virtually Ever After**

• **PulseTV** Instead of the overused slogan claiming the widest selection of products on the face of the planet, PulseTV boasts a highly concentrated list of specialized videos. And no, I don't mean porn. I mean tapes like the Zapruder film of the Kennedy assassination, *How to Irritate People* by Monty Python's John Cleese, and the legendary *Nice Shot!* golf instruction video with Jack Nicklaus. There are twenty-three categories. If one fits your site, register with this outstanding program. You will earn 20 percent on all sales. A unique advantage to the Pulse Affiliate Network (PAN) is that it tracks your onetime referred customers so that you get credited on purchases they make at any time in the future regardless of whether they come directly from your site. In other words, you get 20 percent of their lifetime sales volume at PulseTV! Checks are mailed monthly with no minimum commission requirement.

**www.pulsetv.com/pan index.html**

• **SendWine.com** For your gourmet visitors, there's a bottle of wine waiting to be recommended. SendWine.com sells wine in gift sets for business contacts and family members on every type of occasion. There are two affiliate levels: champagne and vintage. Most moderate-volume sites are classified as champagne while higher-volume sites are vintage. SendWine.com determines your affiliate level when you join. In each quarter as a champagne affiliate, you will earn $7 per sale for orders 1 to 15, $10 per sale for orders 16 to 30, and $13 per sale for orders 31 and higher. Checks are mailed quarterly once your commissions exceed $100.

**www.sendwine.com/affiliate.asp**

• **TravelNow.com** Millions of people now book their travel arrangements online. TravelNow.com provides online hotel reservations, car rentals, group travel, and every type of airfare. If you write about your own travel experiences or provide information specific to a certain part of the world, an integrated link to TravelNow.com is a valuable service. You can link to the overall site and let your visitors hunt for items of interest, or you can link directly to a customized search, a specific hotel, or a city directory. You earn 50 percent on all sales. Checks are mailed monthly once your commissions exceed $10.

**affiliate.travelnow.com/new/index.html**

- **Web Cards** One way to promote a website is by mailing a postcard of its homepage to potential visitors. Web Cards prints those postcards in full color with prices starting at $95 for 500 cards. Also, there's no setup fee. Customers just provide their site address and Web Cards goes to the site and makes postcards from the homepage. You earn money on both leads and sales. For every person requesting a free sample, you earn $1. For every product order, you earn 10 percent. Checks are mailed monthly once your commissions exceed $10.
  **www.printing.com/bannerinstructns.htm**

## Affiliate Directories

While I consider the twenty programs in the previous section to be among the best choices, they're not the only ones. Your site may be highly specialized and better suited to products not sold by any of the merchants I presented. If that's the case, or you just want to see what else is out there, spend some time browsing affiliate program directories.

My favorite directory is at **www.clickquick.com**. The site's host, Ryan Adams, worked for a year and a half on banner advertising for a Fortune 1000 company. His experience taught him what works and what doesn't on the Internet. He ranks various affiliate programs with one to four dollar signs, giving you an instant idea for how well a program stacks up with its competitors. The well-designed site and Ryan's researched, in-depth profiles of affiliate programs make ClickQuick a must-visit site for anybody serious about making money as an affiliate.

Another good directory is at **www.sitecash.com**. It includes a backgrounder on how affiliate programs work, how to choose the right ones, and pitfalls to avoid. SiteCash ranks sites from one to five stars based on ease of use and rate of return.

ClickQuick and SiteCash offer the most information with the least amount of advertising. There are many more affiliate directories, all similar in that they are as much about enrolling you in the programs to which they belong as they are about helping you find the programs that are right for your site. Still, you will find a lot to think about if you can see through the bright advertising.

A long list of programs in every category is updated regularly at **www.associateprograms.com**. Last time I checked, there were 1,200 programs to choose from! For even more ideas, go to **www.associate-it.com**, where you'll find a speedy Yahoo-like interface.

## Affiliate Networks

You saw among my listing of affiliate leaders that some merchants belong to networks that manage their affiliate programs for them. It's a convenient way to bring more business to their sites without devoting an entire department to tracking commissions and cutting checks.

Affiliate networks are also a convenient way for you to enroll in several merchant programs at the same time. You sign up once with the network, then choose which specific merchants to represent on your site. The network tracks your accumulated commissions for all programs to which you belong, then mails you a single check covering everything. Here are three affiliate networks you should consider:

- **BeFree** You'll find more than forty merchants in the BeFree network, including heavyweights like barnesandnoble.com and Goto.com. The company has signed up major sites as affiliates, too. You might be surprised to know that the Lycos search engine works with merchants through BeFree. Last I checked, BeFree logged 250 transactions per second. That's a lot of buying going on. Wouldn't you like to be part of it?
  **www.befree.com**
- **Commission Junction** You'll find more than fifty merchants at Commission Junction, all selling products through more than 20,000 affiliates. There are mainstream companies like Fingerhut and eclectic companies like Kaesona, a kaleidoscope shop. After announcing its goal of being the first network with one million affiliates, Commission Junction offered a program that pays sites for referring new affiliates. You earn $1 per affiliate plus 5 percent of the commissions earned by that affiliate.
  **www.cj.com**

• **LinkShare** Here's the company that started it all. LinkShare was the first to coordinate e-commerce partnerships between merchants and websites—even before the partnerships were called affiliate programs. You'll find more than two hundred merchants at LinkShare, many of whom are among the best-known companies on the Web. With names like Borders.com, Cyberian Outpost, Dell, Disney, FAO Schwarz, Hickory Farms, JCPenney, Reader's Digest, The Sharper Image, and Virtual Vineyards, LinkShare offers you some excellent moneymaking opportunities. It also offers you a way to make money by referring new affiliates. You earn 50 cents for each person who registers with LinkShare and $1.50 for every product somebody buys. The LinkShare affiliate management panel is sleek and easy to use. It displays a customizable report on the top page and a simple 1, 2, 3 approach to getting started. It even creates the links for you, which are ready to be dropped right onto your website. If you're going to join just one affiliate network, this is it.
**www.linkshare.com**

## Choosing the Right Programs

As you can see, there are hundreds of affiliate programs available to you. Combined, they offer every type of product imaginable with various commission schedules. How can you choose which ones are right for your site?

Most important, consider the editorial focus of your site. If you offer your visitors information about pets and babies, then pet and baby products are the obvious choices for you. In addition to that, you could offer books and maybe some videos. It's probably safe to skip the travel sites and dating services. It's not that people with pets and babies don't travel or date, but that they don't expect to pay for those services at a site about pets and babies.

Once you've determined the types of products that will appeal to your visitors, then you can begin narrowing down the merchants that offer those products. You'll want to keep the commission schedule in mind, of course. If two merchants sell the same product at the same price but one will pay you 5 percent more than the other, you should choose the higher-paying merchant. However, there may be more to the story. After looking into the details, you could find that the higher-paying merchant offers little support and a crummy interface for shoppers who will come from your site. All things considered, the lower-paying merchant may end up being your better choice.

**Maybe Vacations Fit Your Site**

That last point is worth expanding upon. Every product you offer is a reflection of your judgment. Your reputation is not worth a few nickels. Make sure you are thoroughly familiar with the merchants you're recommending and that you feel comfortable buying from them yourself. In fact, do just that if possible. Buy your mom some flowers from a flower shop you're considering, buy a book online, get your credit report, book a flight, buy a pair of socks, choose a new picture for your bedroom, and so on. You'll not only save money buying these items online, you'll greatly increase your credibility with visitors. Your own experience will show when you write about the companies. You'll know in advance what your visitors will experience when they click on your product links, and that will help you determine the best place to put those product links. It isn't necessary to try every single product you offer on your website, but you should certainly know every single store affiliated with your site.

You know that repeat sales are a key part of any business. Satisfied customers will return, enjoy themselves again, and recommend your business to others. Your business in this case is a website. An important part of your website is your product line and how well you integrate it into your content. If visitors consistently find excellent products offered to them at just the moment they are interested in buying such products, they will be thrilled and will come to see you as a trustworthy consumer filter. "Hey, he recommended this book so it must be good," or "Let's see what books she recommends on this topic" are the kinds of things you want people saying about you and your site.

Building that kind of reputation takes consistent quality. Make sure you choose companies that will provide it. There's nothing worse than getting an e-mail from a visitor who followed one of your links into a nightmare of overcharged credit cards, undelivered products, and disconnected phones. Aside from being bad for business, it's just plain unfair.

There are billions of places your visitors could have gone on the Web, but they came to your site. Treat them with the gratitude they deserve by offering carefully chosen products from superb merchants.

# Selling Products at Your Site

Finding appropriate merchants and selecting appropriate products are important parts of making money online. But you still have to sell those products to your site visitors. You are the sales rep. Your site is your store and it's up to you to arrange the virtual shelves attractively, greet people with a smile, and make them feel comfortable browsing around.

## Tailor Offerings to Your Content

People will buy from you because you place products that they are thinking about in front of them for immediate purchase. You are not going to inform anybody of the mere existence of Amazon.com. They already know. They aren't going to click a button on your site to go to the opening page of Amazon.com's storefront. That's no service to them at all.

What they will click, however, is a link to a book about growing roses that is placed at the top of an article about rose gardens. They will click on a book about Japan from within your travel essay on Kyoto. They will click on the *Star Wars* soundtrack placed at the bottom of your movie review. Integrating products this closely with your content is the way to successful affiliate sales.

Remember that people can buy the products you offer them at any time in a number of places. You're pushing a great deal on a Dell computer? They can buy a computer down the street or go directly to Dell. You offer a pretty gift pack from Hickory Farms? They can get the same thing at their mall. You're recommending a vacation through TravelNow.com? Their personal travel agent is only a phone call away. You suggest a credit card through NextCard? Their mailbox is filled every day with credit card offers.

When you think about it, you're not offering products at all. You're offering the service of having found the exact product your visitors want at a good price. It's the convenience of being able to trust your recommendations and have the right product show up on their doorstep that will make people buy repeatedly from your site.

**Your Site Should Find the Exact Right Products**

To help you tailor your product offerings to your content, I suggest making a list of the merchants with whom you're partnered. Under each one, write the main products that they offer. Keep the list near your computer. As you create new content for your site such as an article, movie review, or recipe, ask yourself what products are related. Look over the list, then visit the relevant merchants to find specific items of interest to people viewing the content.

If you do this for every new page you post to your website, you will soon have an enormous "product catalog" spread discretely among valuable information. I try to include at least one link that can earn money per page. It doesn't need to be an eyesore, just a quiet link that people will see as a helpful service to get a product that's of interest.

## Use Text Links Most of the Time

You've seen banners and buttons and flashing lights everywhere you go on the Web. Do you bother looking anymore? Probably not. Most people I spoke with in researching this book said that they just read text when they are browsing the Web. A good percentage of them even set their browsers to only display text. They never even see the banners and buttons.

You can show pictures of the products you sell or advertisements for the merchants you do business with, just don't overdo it. I've been to sites that look like business card bulletin boards at a gas station. Grids of buttons all compete with each other in a confusing storm of offers. That's no service to anybody.

If you're going to offer lots of products, do it in the appropriate places (as you read in the last section), and do it discreetly. Text links allow you to accomplish both tasks easily.

Text links are small and load quickly. They do not distract visitors from the content they're trying to absorb from your site. Ten colored buttons stacked in a 5 × 2 grid at the top of your article are eyesores and take a long time to load. Ten text links in a shaded box are discreet and load instantly.

When highlighting a single product, a picture is a good idea. If you're reviewing a book at your website, you should show its cover and a link to buy it. Same with travel writing. If I'm reading about your cruise to Baja, show me a picture of the ship with a link to where I can buy the same cruise. Don't feel the need to show me ten different cruise companies in full color who offer similar packages. I don't want to think about this. You think about it and show me what you consider to be the best value for my money. Show me only that one.

## Use Consistent Placement

Try to place product links in the same area on each page with similar content. I've found that a shaded box of links at the top and bottom of my articles results in a lot of hits. People know when they read an article at my site that it will contain a box full of related products right up front and again at the end when they've finished the article. The consistent placement makes it easy for them to find the products, and they know that whatever is in the shaded box is for sale. There's nothing misleading. As an added bonus, the text of the article is left unblemished by links. That makes for easier reading, which seems like an important consideration in an article. The top of an article from my website is shown on page 96.

Notice that this technique should be limited to pages with similar content, articles in my example. Some of your content

Email Jason Kelly | About Jason Kelly | **JasonKelly** | The Neatest Little Guides | Free Sample of The NeatSheet

**Y2K** **$Mags** Instant Stock Alerts Click for Yahoo! Pager **The Fed** **Soc Sec**

**Investments | Movies | Making Money Online | Politics | Travel | Store**
NeatNet Directory | Make This Your Homepage | Recommend It

## Use Stop Loss Orders for Internet Stocks

**Profit!** Stocks Mentioned | *The NeatSheet* $Mags | *The Neatest Guide* *The Gorilla Game* *Every Investor's Guide to High Tech Stocks* *The Secrets of Investing in Tech*

You've undoubtedly read that anybody investing in Internet companies is crazy. The valuations are out of whack, the companies make no money, it's a bubble, and so on. Even the cover of the January 25, 1999 *U.S. News and World Report* read "The Internet Stock Bubble: When Will It Pop?" The inevitable conclusion was that nobody knows, but we can sure learn a lot from the way people bid up stocks related to radio in the 1920s.

Give me a break. The only people complaining about the "bubble" are the ones who haven't felt its soapy profits. Yes, **Amazon.com** has reached ridiculous prices in the past few weeks and has started falling. So has **Yahoo!** and **@Home** and the rest of the gang. But some of us were brave enough to ride the stocks as they reached those ridiculous heights. Who cares whether prices rise from bubbles or the strongest fundamentals the world has ever seen? Not me. The only reason any of us ever buy a stock is because we believe we can sell it for a higher price later on. Whether that higher price comes from everybody loving the balance sheet or just loving the company's ads is irrelevant. Buying low and selling high — or buying high and selling much higher — works no matter why the market drove the price upward.

The only issue for all these soothsayers is when to sell. Only a madman complains about his investments growing in value. The intelligent investor simply slaps a stop loss order on the astronomically priced stock and waits. It's worked wonders for me and I intend to keep using it throughout this wavy Internet price patter.

Here's how it works.

might be better suited to a different method of product presentation. For instance, a weather report might use a product link from within the text, like this:

> You can track local weather yourself using the same software I use. It's called **WinWeather** and is available for $19.95 from Beyond.com. You'll receive hourly reports and forecasts, satellite images, and even ski updates!

How's that for a discreet, relevant product placement? If somebody is reading about weather on your site, they're interested in weather. They might just want to spend $19.95 to know more about the weather. The WinWeather link should take the customer directly to the product listing at Beyond.com. Some people recommend that you also link the Beyond.com part of the sentence to the company's homepage. I don't think that's necessary because anybody going to the product listing will be able to get to the homepage in a single click. Don't force your visitors to make a choice when it isn't necessary. When there's only one item to click, they know exactly what to do.

In this case, your consistency might be that you place the same three-sentence ad at the bottom of every weather report. Your loyal weather readers will come to expect it, and later, when you discover a new product or an additional product, you can add it to the same area.

## Consolidate Products into a Store

While weaving your products into your content is an excellent service to your visitors, it does bring with it the disadvantage of scattering your store among hundreds or even thousands of pages. To see everything you sell, your visitors would need to click to every page on your site. Nobody is going to do that just for the shopping. Plus, what if somebody reads one of your pages and sees a product link that interests them but can't look at it right away? They might forget where they saw it and be unable to purchase it later.

To address these concerns, I recommend that you maintain an actual storefront somewhere on your site. In it, arrange your products by their common traits, and show where visitors can read your editorial content related to the product. A simple table is the best way to format the listing. You can see the way the top section of mine looks by turning the page.

You are not creating the storefront with the expectation that people will come to your site just to browse your store. Face it, your store will never compete with the likes of Amazon.com or JCPenney.com. It's not supposed to. If people get on the Web to engage in a full-blown shopping excursion, they're going to do it at a dedicated retail merchant, not at your simple site store.

You are creating the storefront as a convenient way for visitors to see the many varied products you offer in relation to your

Email Jason Kelly | About Jason Kelly | **JasonKelly** | The Neatest Little Guides | Free Sample of The NeatSheet

**Y2K** | **$Mags** | Instant Stock Alerts Click for Yahoo! Pager | **The Fed** | **Soc Sec**

**Investments | Movies | Making Money Online | Politics | Travel | Store**
NeatNet Directory | Make This Your Homepage | Recommend It

Ant-Mart Gifts Health Magazines MM Online Software Star Wars Travel

## Jason Kelly's Web Store

**Ants | Clinton | Current Events | Future Planning | History | Holiday | Investing | Web Design | Web Marketing**

### Current Events

| Item | Where Recommended |
|---|---|
| *The Age of Terrorism* | Movie Review |
| *After The First Death* | Movie Review |
| *American Extremists* | Movie Review |
| *Target USA* | Movie Review |

### History

| Item | Where Recommended |
|---|---|
| *Behind The Mask* (about the first Queen Elizabeth) | Movie Review |
| *Elizabeth* | Movie Review |
| *The First Elizabeth* | Movie Review |
| *Life of Elizabeth* | Movie Review |

### Investing

| Item | Where Recommended |
|---|---|
| *The Neatest Little Guide to Mutual Fund Investing* | Book Description |
| *The Neatest Little Guide to Stock Market Investing* | Book Description |
| *The Neatest Little Guie to Personal Finance* | Book Description |
| *The Electronic Day Trader* | Investment Articles |
| *Every Investor's Guide to High-Tech Stocks* | Investment Articles |
| *The Gorilla Game* | Investment Articles |

content. The added service that you provide in your store is a link to content related to each article. People love that. They want to read about cars they're considering, hot new computers, great books, lovely CDs, and fabulous vacations. In your store, show them the products in a logical arrangement and show them where they can read more about each product or about something related to the product.

Similar to your main storefront, consider assembling what I call "product pods." These are products connected by a theme. You see this technique in action at malls and stores every day. Remember when *Star Wars Episode I* was released in May 1999? Every store in the country placed a Star Wars table inside the front door. Books, calendars, toys, and posters greeted customers who had spent weeks anticipating the movie's release. That Star Wars table was a product pod.

If you write regularly about a certain theme and collect a sizable offering of products around it, create a product pod for that theme. Give it a special page where those products are highlighted with extra commentary and more graphics than usual. Point to your product pods from your related site content and also from your main storefront.

A product pod is convenient for people interested in the theme, and it's also an easy way for you to make sure you're always pointing visitors to the most current products. For example, think back to the WinWeather offer you read about on page 96. That software will certainly be updated in the future. What if the tornado article you wrote on June 1, 2000, remains on your site for an extended period of time and links to version two of the software? When the software is updated to version 3.0 in 2001, your visitors will still be directed to the old software or, worse, a dead link because the software store will have killed the old product page.

If your tornado article links instead to a weather product pod that's regularly updated with the newest products, the problem is solved. Now, you have only one page on which to update products instead of the many that point to a specific product listing. If all pages related to weather point to your weather store, that weather store is all that needs to be kept current.

## Consolidate Merchants into a Mall

Just as consolidating products is a good service to your visitors, so is consolidating your merchants. A simple columnar listing is fine, along with your endorsement at the top. For example, "I am proud to support the following online merchants." You might want to get fancier and include a one- or two-sentence description of each merchant along with why you like them.

You'll find a good mall of merchants at **www.shopweb.net**. Notice how stores are grouped by category and arranged in a simple manner.

## The Best Online Shopping Index

### SHOPWEB.NET

Click on the links below for safe online internet shopping

**Books and Software**

- Barnesandnoble.com
- Amazon.com® Books
- Amazon.co.uk -in the UK
- Borders.com Books
- Barnesandnoble.com Software

**Music and Videos**

- CDnow©/MusicBlvd
- Bn.com Music
- CD Universe®
- CD World Entertainment
- Reel.com® Movies

**Department Stores**

- Jcrew.com Clothes
- Paul Fredrick
- JCPenney Online Shopping
- WalMart Online
- dELiA*s Teen clothes

Your merchant mall is a good place to take advantage of affiliate search features. Many affiliates offer search boxes that you can place on your site. Visitors type in the product they're seeking and are taken to a list of results at the merchant site. You earn a credit for anything purchased as a result of the search.

Most of the time, search boxes are annoying. Few people want to stop reading and type in a search query. You're trying to minimize the need to make decisions at your website. Whenever possible, you give people only one link to click so that even the slightest instinctive reaction toward it results in a click. With two links, you've lost half your audience. With three, another quarter. With a search box that's not even multiple choice but forces the user to actually think of what to type, you've lost everybody but that nerd you hated in high school.

In your mall, however, the situation changes. Anybody stopping by that section of your website is interested in the merchants you recommend. They can click on the link and go to the homepage to browse, but you could save them a step by providing the merchant's search feature directly from your mall.

# 6 Selling Your Own Products and Services

You can make money any way you want with your new website. You might have created it with the express purpose of taking your existing business online or to create a whole new income stream. Either way, the option of selling your own products and services is something you should consider. It's a lot more work than selling other merchants' products and services as an affiliate, but it can lead to more money as well.

## Advantages and Disadvantages

The biggest advantage to selling your own products and services is that you will make more money. When you manufacture a machine, bake a cookie, or print your own book, you keep a big profit margin. When you sell somebody else's machine, cookie, or book, you get a small sales commission. The profit difference between the two business models is dramatic. For example, if you sell a $25 book at Amazon.com and keep 15 percent, you get $3.75. If you print the book yourself for $2 and sell it directly to the customer from your Web site, you get $23. A profit difference of $19.25 on a $25 sale is pretty serious. That's why you should consider selling your own products. Yours might not be books, but the same comparisons between commissions and direct selling will apply no matter what you offer the world.

A second advantage is that you keep complete control over your product or service. You determine the packaging, the quality of materials, the method of delivery, and the customer service. Nobody can mistreat your customers.

Running Your Own Business Ain't Easy

The biggest disadvantage is that you keep complete control over your product or service. Yes, while it's a great opportunity to get everything right, it's also a great burden. You will need to track orders, monitor inventory, and collect payment. If there's a problem, the customer will contact you. All the financial risk of making your product and providing your service will fall squarely on your bank account. Inventory is expensive and it takes space. Do you have the money? Do you have the space? Do you have the time to fulfill small orders on a spotty basis? Do you have the resources to fulfill big ones?

These are questions that need to be answered if you're going to offer your own products. Of course, answering them doesn't mean that you must answer them the same way Wal-Mart answers them. It's all right for you to run a low-volume, simple operation out of your garage, with the tracking system being a pad of paper and pencil. As long as your customers are happy and you can handle the business, keep it going.

Just be aware that when you start selling goods online you have become a mail-order company. At that point, your website is one of the smallest parts of your operation. It's the catalog of your products, that's all. A pretty deluxe catalog, but a catalog nonetheless. Managing the rest of your business will be the bigger concern.

That being the case, I recommend that you read a couple of the many books written about mail order. I will spend the rest of this chapter discussing the website portion of your business, but won't go into the details of creating products, warehousing them, record-keeping, and so on.

# What Sells Well Online

Few people are going to buy from your site what they can get from more familiar sites. For instance, if your name is Carl and you open Carl's Computers on the Web to sell new computers directly to consumers, you've got a real battle on your hands. Not only do you need to set up a company that can make and ship computers—which is very hard to do out of your garage—you also need people to choose your website over those of Dell, Gateway, and others. On your own or even with a small staff of employees, you will have a tough time outrunning established direct-selling computer companies. The main reason is that people can already get computers at dozens of places everybody knows about.

## Unique Products That Are Hard to Find

If, however, you decide to open Carl's Crustacean Artwork on the Web to sell one-of-a-kind decorations, you'll have a better chance. You fill a pin-sized niche, exactly what the Web is best at. As an added bonus, your niche happens to be with products that aren't easy to come by. When was the last time you wandered into Target's crustacean art aisle? Never. You have to search high and low for it, and so do other crustacean art buyers. Once that specific consumer group discovers Carl's Crustacean Artwork on the Web, word will spread quickly among crustacean lovers, and you will enjoy a brisk business. It might not be high-volume by corporate standards, but it could be enough to support you and your family.

The beauty of the Internet is that it makes searching so much easier. What used to take days of phone books and dialing and classified ads can now be accomplished in a few minutes. Listed appropriately, Carl's Crustacean Artwork would be found immediately by any search engine looking for the term "crustacean artwork." There aren't a lot of competitors anywhere, so folks in Miami looking for a picture of a crab for their kitchen will be willing to buy it from a mail-order company in San Francisco.

Look at the products you are considering offering online. Search the Web yourself to see if others offer them. If it's a well-established business category like books, software, or toys, consider the affiliate route to selling products. Let another company face the risks and expenses while you keep a commission. If you don't find much online to compete with your product, that's a good sign. If you don't see your product in stores around town, that's a good sign. If your friends and acquaintances have said to you on a number of occasions that "I can't find a bamboo pencil case," and you are thinking of selling bamboo pencil cases, that is a good sign.

Note that niches exist even within well-defined product categories. For instance, Jack Moore of Austin, Texas, is a freelance commercial animator who decided that kids might like to read stories on their computers. Using his animation skills, he created interactive stories that are 30 to 35 pages in length with black and white line drawings, picture captions, and an audio file to tell the story. Children can even color in the line drawings themselves and save their own creative contribution to the story. Jack named his company Tellitagan and sells the stories at **www.tellitagan.com**. You get four stories for $12.95 including postage. Each additional story on the same CD-ROM is $2. Bookselling might be a crowded market, but Jack's stories are unique and you can only get them from Tellitagan.

I suppose the same can be said of Carl's Crustacean Artwork. Home decorating is a crowded market, but the crustacean niche isn't. Carl would probably offer products that aren't available anywhere else.

Anaconda at **www.anaconda.net** is another good example of a company occupying a niche within an established category. It sells software that helps Amazon.com affiliates make more money. The software category sounds far too mainstream for a small company to make money. At first blush, it looks like they're competing with the likes of Microsoft, Lotus, and Symantec. But they're not. Nobody else makes software that does what Anaconda's does. That's a strong niche in an established category.

Just when you thought everything that can be done with a pen has been done, along comes DeBerry Products with its Light

Writer. This ballpoint pen features a built-in LED that illuminates the page so that you can write in a darkened room. The product is perfect for movie reviewers, policemen, pilots, and others who need to write in the dark. Have you ever seen this product in a store? Not likely. But you can get it on the Web at **www.lightwriter.com**.

Emulate these stories when coming up with your products. Make them unique and offer them to the whole world at your website.

## Timely-Information Products

Second only to the Web's ease of searching is its timely information delivery. Thanks to the Internet, I know the headlines before the newspaper ever arrives. In some businesses, people will pay for that speedy information.

Ordinary news is available everywhere for free. However, in specialized niches, you can charge for information that others need. Investors, business owners, and researchers are accustomed to paying for information. Using the Web, you can deliver such information quickly and affordably.

The fast-changing world of legislation created an opportunity for one company to sell up-to-the-minute news. Legicrawler at **www.legicrawler.com** offers the latest information on state, federal, and international legislation. For businesses concerned with environmental regulations, tax statutes, and such, the service is worth paying for.

You may have access to a similar niche that you track closely. Running a subscription-based site is more difficult than a product site because you need to create a log-in system that verifies the paid status of your members. You'll need to hire a programmer to help with that.

However, if your information is offered through a paper newsletter, e-mail, or fax service, it's a regular product that you can market and sell like others on your site. This may not be the best way to take advantage of speedy Web delivery, but it can still work if you occupy that all-important specialized niche. Just making your product easy to find on the Internet can be enough.

For instance, I've written *The NeatSheet*, my monthly

investment newsletter, for years. By providing a free sample at my website along with subscription information and a list of key features, I've been able to create a steady stream of subscriptions with little effort. The Web has allowed me to stop mass mailings, to point everybody seeking a sample issue to the website, where the sample doesn't cost them or me a dime, and to automate the entire product query process. Some subscribers like to receive their newsletter via e-mail, but the vast majority still prefer a paper product delivered the old-fashioned way with a stamp—even if they discovered the newsletter online.

This goes to show that you can market an information product on the Internet without taking advantage of instantaneous online delivery.

## Web-Specific Products

Products related to the Web sell well on the Web. It makes sense, right? Anybody online is prequalified to be interested in a product made for people who get online. E-mail enhancements, website software, tracking programs, and anything else related to the Internet will have a good chance at being successful when sold online.

Alco Blom saw a need for people to organize their favorite Web destinations and all the passwords and log-in IDs that they accumulate. So he wrote two programs for Macintosh users to address the need. *URL Manager Pro* takes care of the websites while *Web Confidential* handles all the passwords. The products are sold at a modest price from their websites at **www.url-manager.com** and **www.web-confidential.com**. You'll see when visiting the sites that all they do is present information about the products and sell them. That's it. There's no reason for a person to spend hours clicking from page to page. But when somebody searches for a way to manage their URLs or organize their passwords, they'll find Alco's sites, try the software, and probably choose to buy.

If you have an idea for software or another tool that can improve the online experience, start selling it! There's no better place for people to buy it than within the medium it's supposed to improve.

The usual approach to selling online software products is to offer your program on a trial basis for thirty days. After that, the program will not work. Another method is to offer a stripped-down version for free. To get the full capabilities, people must pay for an upgrade. These techniques are effective because visitors to your site can try before they buy. It removes any doubts they have before purchasing and keeps your customer service needs low. Few people will call with complaints if they tried the product before buying.

**Software Sells Well Online**

Another great advantage of selling software over the Internet is that costs are incredibly cheap. You won't need inventory and you'll never ship anything in a box. People pay you with a credit card, then they download the product over the Web. What could be easier?

Actually, there is something that could be easier. You know now that designing and building a website is hard work. It's also work that is increasingly important as every business in the world gets connected. If you enjoyed designing your website, you might enjoy designing others. Because you offer a service out of your home, there is nothing to manage but your time and marketing. It's about as low-risk as your own business gets because there's nothing invested in products that may not sell.

Web design isn't the only Internet-related service you can offer through a website. Online marketing, offline promotions, content creation, and hundreds of other Internet business support services lend themselves to being sold online. For small, one-person operations the deals usually happen over e-mail. You do the work, fine-tune it to your client's satisfaction, send an invoice, and receive a check in the mail.

## Cheap Products

People expect to save money online. If you sell something cheaper than people can get anywhere else, that's appealing to lots of customers. Such a business can be difficult because competitors will slash prices and pretty soon everybody will be living on margins so thin you can paint them on. This is particularly the case with commodity products, where the item is identical no matter where it's purchased. In that circumstance, price is the only differentiation. As soon as somebody offers your product cheaper, your advantage is gone.

Still, if you have the ability to offer the lowest price on the planet, do it boldly from your website. Get it onto the search engines and into a few print articles that you sell 33-cent stamps for 30 cents, ten 40-watt light bulbs for $1, name-brand jeans for $10, airfare to Nepal for $100, heart transplants for $1,000, or new homes along the beach for $10,000. Whatever it is that you sell cheap, the Internet is ready to get the word out.

## Taking Orders and Getting Paid

No matter what you sell, you've got to take orders and get paid. For some services, the process may be as simple as receiving an e-mail request for work to be done and sending a final invoice when the work is completed. That's the simplest scenario and anybody with an e-mail account has the capability.

Far more common, however, is the situation where you display your product, service, or list of products and services. Your potential customers choose what they want and make their purchases. All of that sounds fine until you realize that you're doing this over the Internet. There's no customer standing in front of you while you push buttons on a cash register. Taking the order and getting paid takes on a new dimension at your website.

As you cruise around the Internet, you'll see an enormous range of solutions. Sophisticated sites like Amazon.com allow customers to enter their shipping and credit card information one time and then just click the items they want for automatic ordering and payment. Other sites, like Allison's Cookies, don't offer anything more sophisticated than a page showing the company phone number and mailing address. If you want the product, you write your order on a piece of paper and drop it in the mail with a check.

You'll probably want something between those two extremes.

While people don't expect every small site to compete with the likes of Amazon.com, they do expect to be able to actually order and pay online. That's not to say that you will immediately be classified as amateur if your site does not accept online ordering and payment, but you might lose a few orders because of it.

When confronted with the challenge of taking orders and getting paid, I tried doing it myself. I created forms to collect order information and tried setting up online credit card processing. Before long, there were so many parties involved in trying to make my website work that nobody was accountable for the fact that it didn't work. My hosting service blamed my credit card company who blamed my programming skills. Just in case they were right about my shortcomings, I hired a professional Web programmer to fix everything. Two months and lots of money later, the site still couldn't accept orders and process payments. Customers had to call on the phone to buy my products.

Learn from my mistakes. Unless you are establishing a full-time business online, don't try taking orders and accepting payment at your own website. It is costly, far too complex for you to administer while also running your business, and not worth the few percentage points added to your profit margin. I have found a much better alternative for you. But first . . .

## Get a Merchant Credit Card Account

Before I present my better alternative, I want to discuss the importance of getting a merchant credit card account. No matter what you sell online or how you intend to sell it, the ability to accept credit cards is crucial. You are physically distant from your customers. There is no more convenient or trusted way to pay over long distances than the credit card. Everybody has one and everybody is accustomed to being able to use it.

What? You Don't Take Orders Online?

Just imagine yourself visiting a website that sells the antique vase you've had your heart set on for years. There's no online ordering capability, so you call the phone number. They take your order and you say that you'll put it on your credit card. Nope, they say, you must pay with a check. What's more, they won't ship until they've received your check in the mail and it has been deposited into their account. What a hassle. You now need to copy down the company's mailing address, get out your checkbook, write out the check, put it in the envelope, find a stamp, and mail it. Weeks later, your vase finally arrives.

Buying with a credit card is so much better for everybody concerned. It speeds the transaction along and shows that your business is ready for prime time.

The good news is that getting a merchant credit card account for your business has become quite simple. With the proliferation of small businesses and home-based businesses, banks have become less stringent on the requirements for accepting credit cards. Most merchant companies say that 99 percent of all applications are accepted.

There are hundreds of companies that can establish a merchant credit card account for you. Some good places to start looking are Cardservice International at **www.cardservice.com**, Data Transfer Associates at **www.datatransfer.com**, and eCardNet at **www.ecardnet.com**. Each site answers common questions about merchant accounts and presents a simple form for you to submit. You'll hear back quickly and could be ready to accept cards within a week.

You'll be able to choose between an account that allows you to accept only Visa and MasterCard, or one that allows you to accept those plus American Express and Discover. You can also sign up for additional cards, but these four are the most commonly used. Nearly everybody has a Visa or Mastercard, but many people prefer using AmEx and Discover. The capability to accept those cards isn't necessary for business, although you might be surprised at the number of people who are happy to hear, "Sure, I take American Express."

With any merchant account, you'll pay a discount rate, a transaction fee, and a monthly fee. The discount rate is the amount of the receipt that the credit card company keeps. It's usually between 1 and 3 percent. Transaction fees are between 10 and 40 cents per transaction. Monthly fees are between $10 and $40. So, on a $100 order, you might only collect $97.10 after a

2.5 percent discount rate is collected and you pay a 40-cent transaction fee.

Your merchant company will give you the choice between buying or renting a credit card terminal like the kind you've seen in gas stations or processing software. The monthly rental for either one is usually around $30 and the purchase price is anywhere from $400 to $1,200. For a Web business, the software makes more sense. You'll be amazed at the number of people who will e-mail their credit card information. Being able to copy that directly into your credit card authorization software is a real time-saver. The software also automatically keeps a detailed record of your transaction history. With a terminal, you need to type all numbers in manually and there is no detailed record of your transactions.

When a customer e-mails or calls, you enter their name and sometimes their address, credit card information, and amount of sale. The software dials a toll-free number over your computer modem and returns either an acceptance or denial in seconds. If accepted, the money is deposited into your bank account within three business days. You can also batch transactions together for faster processing. Rather than authorize thirty orders separately, you can batch them together for one phone call that processes all thirty orders.

Once you're established with a merchant credit card account, your business should increase by about 35 percent. That's according to the industry, and I've also experienced that myself. In a room of people listening to a product pitch, the ability to accept credit cards does boost volume by about one third. It works the same on your website. Those little credit card graphics are a quick way of saying that if a visitor wants something they see, they can get it just by typing in a few numbers.

## Get a Toll-free Phone Number and Voicemail

No matter how you intend to sell your products and services, get a toll-free phone number. Its mere presence on a website comforts people who feel that online transactions are mysterious at best and suspect at worst. A good percentage of your business will come over the phone, which will be easy for you to handle because you now accept credit cards.

Getting a toll-free number is a snap, and they cost less than $10 per month. The best number to get is an 800 number, but 888 and 877 might be your only choices. If so, choose 888. I have found when conducting radio interviews that when people hear the phrase “toll-free” they automatically dial 800 even if you emphatically say 888. With so many 888 numbers in use, the situation is changing but it’s still better to have the 800. The number that people are least familiar with is 877. It doesn’t sound toll-free; it sounds like an area code. With toll-free numbers in such high demand, there might be other choices by the time you read this. Do your best to get 800.

You can get a toll-free number from your current long-distance carrier or any of the big three. Call AT&T at 888-928-8932, Sprint at 800-877-4646, or WorldCom at 888-926-6496. You will choose your number, then provide a regular phone number to which your toll-free callers will be directed. This could be your home office, mobile phone, or any other phone. When a customer dials the toll-free number, the phone you specify will ring.

Keep a stack of order forms near the business phone. When you answer, people are ready to do business, so make sure you’re ready as well. You don’t want to act surprised. One time, I called to order cooking utensils from a website and the person answered, “Hello?”

“Hello, I’d like to buy your cooking utensil set.”

There was a long pause. “You would? . . . Okay, um, let me think what to do next.”

Don’t answer your phone that way. Be prepared for callers and have your order forms ready for action. Remember the factors that have made your own phone-ordering experiences good and copy those factors. It’s no mystery. Be friendly, efficient, and accurate. People will be so impressed just to have reached a human instead of a forty-option menu tree that they’ll already be on your side. The slightest effort to be professional will leave your callers feeling good.

Here's a final tip: get voicemail on your business line. It's clearer than answering machines, and it can take other calls while you're talking to a customer. Do not rely on call waiting because it's rude to the customer on the line and makes you look amateurish. When was the last time you called a mail-order company and had the sales rep suddenly interrupt your order with, "Oh, I've got another call. Just a sec?" Hopefully, never. Don't do it to your callers either.

You can get voicemail through your local phone company or from other companies listed under "voicemail" in the yellow pages.

## Sell Through an Online Store

I promised an easy way for you to accept orders and collect payment so that you wouldn't need to suffer through months of tech support calls and thousands of dollars trying to enable your website to handle them automatically. Your merchant credit card account is only part of that system. Having it lets you accept credit cards as payment, but you still need to figure out how to do it online.

The easy way is to use an existing online store. One of the most popular is Yahoo Store at **store.yahoo.com**. For only $100 per month you can list up to fifty items. The interface is so simple that you just use your regular Web browser to build a storefront, list products, specify prices, and so on. You can design the store to integrate with your website or come up with an entirely different look. Yahoo will even recommend designers in your area if you want help creating a professional image. Yahoo Store is home to big names like Ben & Jerry's, Frederick's of Hollywood, NASA, *Rolling Stone*, and Strouds.

Visitors to your site will click to your store, which can have an address of www.yourname.com or store.yahoo.com/yourname. They will browse your products and place orders. You receive orders in one of four ways: viewing your account at Yahoo store, downloading a database file of orders for copying into your current ordering system, having Yahoo fax orders to you, or by running your own server to receive orders in real time. You can change which method you use at any time. Faxes are simple for low-volume businesses while the database might be better for high-volume.

The Yahoo Store shopping basket is one of the best around. You can specify any properties you want in your items, not just sizes and colors. Sale prices and quantity discounts are no problem. You can even build in a cross-selling feature so that when customers order one item the system will suggest related items they might want to order. For instance, if a customer just bought a camping stove, he might also want some insect repellent and a backpack.

Credit card payments are processed online using your existing merchant account. Yahoo Store will help you set up an account, but the last time I checked, their prices were much higher than what you'll find at the three sites I mentioned on page 110. So, bring your own merchant account when you sign up with Yahoo Store.

Yahoo Store does have competitors, the best of which is at **www.icat.com**. The iCat Web Store is built and managed using your browser. You can update your design at any time, add or delete products, check orders, and so on as easily as you can with Yahoo. The price is a bit less, too. Up to ten products will run you only $10 per month or $100 per year. Up to fifty products will run you only $50 per month or $500 per year, half the price of Yahoo.

**It's Easy to Partner with an Online Store**

I've heard from users that the Yahoo store is the better choice because of the promotional push you'll get by being part of the popular Yahoo site. That doesn't hold a lot of water in my opinion. Marketing is always up to you, and you'll learn some excellent ways to go about it in Chapter 7. I suggest that you examine each service and make your decision based on the interfaces and costs. After all, if you have only five products to sell, Yahoo will cost you $1,200 per year while iCat will cost you only $100. The $1,100 savings is compelling.

Unless you've gone through the nightmare of trying to coordinate a functional online store, you'll have trouble appreciating either of these solutions. You won't spend half your week on phone calls to credit card companies, hosting service tech support, banks, programmers, and anybody else they suggest you call. You'll just list your products and fill orders. Everything will work without you ever needing to understand how.

## Sell Through an Online Auction

Another simple way to use another company's technology to sell your products is through an auction site. You list your product, specify the minimum bid, indicate who pays for shipping, and determine the duration of the auction. You can also provide a description and photo of your product.

People will then have the opportunity to bid on your product. As long as your minimum bid is high enough to make the price worth your while, you have nothing to worry about. You might get more than you expected. If people bid on the product, you'll have a buyer when the auction closes. They provide payment with a credit card or other method mutually agreeable, then you ship the product.

You only pay a few dollars to list your product, and at some places it's free. For less than the cost of a fast-food meal, you can put something up for sale on the Internet. You don't even need to have a website. All you need is a product to sell.

Certain products sell better at online auctions than others. The top categories are antiques and collectibles. Buyers and sellers in those categories are accustomed to dealing, so doing it online is second nature to them. In other categories like books, software, and clothing, sales aren't nearly as brisk.

I have spoken with people in my neighborhood who are making $500 to $1,000 per month by visiting garage sales and antique shows on Sunday, buying items as cheaply as possible, then listing and selling them at online auction sites. One lady had been a junk dealer for years, but there was no Internet, so she didn't sell online. Instead, she held a sale of her own once per month. She displayed all of her items and sat there with a cash box to close deals. Now, over the Internet, she holds sales constantly without needing to be physically present, and she doesn't even keep a website. She consistently turns a 20 percent profit.

Even if an auction isn't your primary method of selling products, it can be a very good complementary method. Perhaps you'll sell 90 percent of your widgets through iCat or Yahoo Store and only 10 percent through an auction site. That 10 percent is worth pursuing, especially since it's so cheap and easy.

The best auction sites are at **auctions.amazon.com**; **www.auctionuniverse.com**; **www.ebay.com**; and **auctions.yahoo.com**. It's either cheap or free to list your items for sale at each location.

## Using Autoresponders to Close Sales

One of the toughest challenges when you're selling a product is providing good customer service. You want to treat everybody with care, but that can be time consuming. Ideally, every inquiry you receive would be handled with a personal response, such as a phone call or an e-mail.

But I've found that with certain products, the questions are always the same. Take cars, for example. When buying a new car, everybody wants to know how many people it seats, the fuel economy, and the price. Always. There will be other questions that are unique to individual buyers, but everybody will want to know those three pieces of information.

It's probably the same with products that you sell. There are a set of questions that every prospect needs answered before they buy. You could answer those questions with a frequently asked questions document, also known as an FAQ. However, an FAQ requires that the user locate the link, go to the page, and scroll through it for information. It's passive and therefore doesn't do much to close sales.

What I have found to be far more effective is an autoresponder. On page 33, I urged you to respond personally to all inquiries. For the most part you should, unless you specifically tell people that you have created a program that will automatically tell them everything they need to know about your product.

The difference is that they understand they're signing up for free automated information. They know that you are not going to personally write the document and deliver it to them. Because they don't expect to hear from you personally, they won't be disappointed. They simply enter their e-mail address in the box that you display and wait for the information to be delivered. If they have questions specifically for you, they can e-mail you directly.

The best program I have found for creating this autoresponse sales system is at **www.aweber.com**. Based on the belief that it takes a prospect seven or more exposures to your product before they buy, the AWeber system allows you to schedule timed deliveries of additional product information.

Your first e-mail to prospects could be an introduction to the benefits of your product. A day later, they would receive an in-depth exploration of the feature that everybody raves about. Perhaps a week after that, another note would arrive reminding the prospect of what they've learned about your product so far, and then showing another nifty aspect of it that no competitor offers. This process can continue to a maximum of seven e-mails spaced between four hours apart and 99 days apart.

When somebody enters their name and e-mail address, both are captured in a database that you can use later. You will also receive a confirmation when a new prospect has requested product information. Best of all, the prospect's name is used on all of your sales messages. For example, the subject of the first e-mail you send might be "Tom Jones, are you satisfied with your flower beds?" The note would then explain to Tom that your company sells flowers with the brightest colors in the solar system. You can specify on the control panel where you create your sales messages exactly how you want your prospect's name to be used. AWeber uses a variable called $NAME that you place in the e-mail subject line or in the text of your notes. The prospect's name appears in its place whenever a message is sent.

**Let the Computer Handle Requests for Info**

The AWeber system costs $15 per month if you pay once a year and $20 per month if you pay monthly. Visit the site to give the system a whirl. As you might guess, you can enter your name and e-mail address to use the very system you're thinking of buying to learn more about how it works. Within seconds, your first note will arrive with your name in the subject. When you purchase the AWeber system online, you will be activated and ready to put the entry boxes on your website within one minute.

# 7 Marketing Your Site

Every business needs customers. If you open a coffee shop, you need people to wander through before they can buy coffee. It's the same with your website. You need people to click there before they can buy anything. Building a site without promoting it will get you nothing but a pretty website to show your friends. After building an excellent site and stocking it with products and services for sale, you need to let the world know about it.

## Get Listed in Top Search Engines

Most people get where they're going online by using a search engine. Surveys by media rating companies say that the number is anywhere from 75 to 85 percent. That means you should be listed in search engines so that when people are searching for sites like yours, they find yours listed.

### Use Meta Tags for Spiders

Some search engines find your site automatically by sending a spider to crawl through and index it. The programs are also known as robots (or just *bots*), but I'll call them spiders here. They are constantly on the lookout for new sites. Unfortunately, they don't always know how to classify your site.

A spider looks at the title of your site and the first paragraph to determine what your site is about. That's not very sophisticated because your first paragraph might not contain words that accurately describe the overall theme of your site. Thus, your collection of ceramic thimbles will never be found because neither the word *thimble* nor *ceramic* appears in the first paragraph. You could always change your page around just for the spiders, but that can be too restrictive.

Instead, you should rely on what are called meta tags. These are special instructions to spiders that tell them a description of your site and a list of keywords that should be used to find it. Your visitors never see the meta tags. They are just HTML code that sits behind the scenes waiting for spiders to visit.

All three of the website design programs that I recommend on page 47 offer the ability to use meta tags at your website. Here's the keyword meta tag information from Amazon.com:

> <META NAME="keywords" CONTENT="amazon.com, amazon books, amazon bookstore, amazon.com books, amazon music, amazon.com music, amazon video, amazon.com video, auctions, amazon auctions, amazon.com auctions, electronics, consumer electronics, gifts, amazon gifts, amazon.com gifts, cards, e-cards, e-mail cards, greeting cards, amazon cards, amazon.com cards, toys, amazon toys, amazon.com toys, games, amazon games, amazon.com games, toys & games, toys and games">

You can see that it's fairly simple. The meta tag "keywords" tells the spider which keywords should be used to find the site. You can use this code at your site by simply replacing the information specific to Amazon.com with information about your site. There are other available meta tags as well, such as title, description, author, and so on, but the keywords are the most important.

Notice the effort that Amazon.com spent covering various ways to say the same thing. Some people will type "amazon toys" while others might search on "amazon.com toys." To get both terms into the search engines, Amazon.com has created keywords for each phrase. You should do the same.

To see how to add meta tags to your site using your design software, look up "meta tags" in the online help.

Once you've finished your tags, use the MetaMedic tool at **www.northernwebs.com**. It will analyze your homepage and show how well you've used meta tags to properly list your site with search engines.

## Submit Your Site to the Engines

While many search engines rely on spiders to find new sites, others require you to submit your site for evaluation and placement in the right category. Because there are so many search engines, some people hire a service to submit their site everywhere.

Such submission services are quick to point out the volume of search engines to which your site will be submitted. I've seen claims of more than 1,500 engines and directories. That sounds fabulous until you realize that nobody has heard of any past the top ten. Say Yahoo to people and they instantly know what you're talking about. Say The Rail to people and they think you're talking about a train trip. I don't see a whole lot of value in having your site listed at The Rail.

However, if you want to check out the submission services to decide for yourself, click over to **www.announceit.com**; **www.netcreations.com/postmaster**; and **www.submit-it.com**. The various packages range in price from $29 for a onetime submission to $499 for ongoing priority placement, which is supposed to be a continual effort to get your site listed at the top of relevant searches.

A better place to get help submitting your site is Robert Woodhead's self-promotion service at **www.selfpromotion.com**. The clever Mr. Woodhead created the first site registration share service after becoming annoyed at the pay services that claim to submit to more search engines than actually exist. Self-Promotion.com takes all the various submission forms from search engines and consolidates them into a customized one that works everywhere. This way, you enter your information only one time to have it registered at multiple locations, sparing you hours of redundant data entry. You can use SelfPromotion.com for free. If you find it to be useful, you pay Mr. Woodhead what you think the service is worth. I was amused to see that one satisfied user enclosed this note with his payment: "You really should be impressed that you're getting money out of me. I NEVER pay for anything, but I am THAT impressed with your site. Keep up the good work or I'll kill you." In addition to Mr. Woodhead's well-designed submission tool, his site features several good articles about website promotion that might just keep you from wasting money.

**You Can Do It Yourself, but It Takes Time**

To save yourself some money and make sure your site is submitted properly, you can do it yourself by going to each search engine and filling out the submission form. Before you do, think long and hard about what it is your site offers visitors. Write on a piece of paper which search terms people are most likely to use when looking for sites like yours. Below that, write a description of your site in fifty words or less. You will need both pieces of information at each site you visit for a listing. People conducting a search can tell which sites were submitted with information created hastily because the descriptions are rough and sometimes there are even misspelled words. These important words that describe your site to the rest of the world will be what determine whether a person clicks or not. So spend a little time getting them right.

After you have your submission information finalized, stop by the biggest search engines and look for the link "Add URL" or "Submit URL" at the bottom of the homepage. Click it and you'll be presented with a form asking for information about your site, including the description and what keywords should find it. You now have those handy and will breeze through the form.

Here are the ten sites that you absolutely must be listed on:

**www.altavista.com**
**www.aol.com/netfind**
**www.excite.com**
**www.hotbot.com**
**www.infoseek.com**

www.looksmart.com
www.lycos.com
www.northernlight.com
www.stpt.com
www.yahoo.com

If you're going to concentrate on a single listing, make it Yahoo. Because it is a hand-indexed site, there are fewer listings per category and the listings tend to be more relevant than what you'll find at other sites. Getting yourself into a Yahoo category can double your traffic.

After submitting to all ten sites, stop by periodically to check your listing. If you can't find it, resubmit. Sometimes your site will be listed in an entirely inappropriate category or not at all. You may find that providing additional comments where possible can help you get listed. My site was never listed at Yahoo until I mentioned to them that it helps people manage their money. Within two weeks, the site was listed and traffic nearly doubled.

To sum up, you can do your site submission yourself to save money, but doing so requires a lot of time. Consider using Self-Promotion.com instead. Because the service is free, there is no risk. You send money only if it works for you. I would avoid the pay-up-front scrvices.

## Rely on Quality to Improve Your Site's Ranking

You've probably noticed that doing a search at any of the major search engines returns somewhere around 279,000 listings. You don't want your site to be number 278,994. Nobody will page through that many options.

Welcome to the never-ending task of improving your site's ranking at the search engines. Entire businesses have sprung up around this one part of Web marketing. The coveted top-ten listings of any subject area are sought after by every company in that field. Some people fight dirty, others bubble to the top in offline promotions, and some just give up this battle and move on to other marketing tactics.

But guess what? For all the energy put into site ranking and all the products available to help you move higher in the list, there's actually not much you can do aside from building a site worth visiting.

You can take some relief in knowing that a well-designed site with valuable information or products will stand out. It will do so because newer search techniques weigh the relevance of sites based on how often they are clicked. If everybody who wants to know about making lemonade eventually ends up at your lemonade site, it will be ranked highly in lemonade searches. You could certainly help it by using meta tags and checking the site's listing every six months or so, but the word-of-mouth and extensive linking that will result from being the best lemonade site on the Web will be reflected in the search engines.

Yahoo, for instance, has real people look over your site. They judge it the same way a potential visitor would. Is it attractive, easy to navigate, and useful in some way? If so on all counts, Yahoo will be doing its visitors a service by listing your site in a prominent place. Conversely, if your site strikes out on all counts, Yahoo will be doing its visitors a service by saving them a click. The site won't be listed.

Some consultants will tell you that the words in your site title are weighted most heavily by search engines. Next, they say to concentrate on getting your keywords into your first paragraph. Do this, do that; change this, change that.

Forget it. What works at one engine is completely irrelevant at another. As important as meta tags are, for instance, they're ignored by Excite. HotBot and Infoseek rely on them almost exclusively. Yahoo prefers sites that it has not only visited but reviewed. Fine-tuning your site to work extremely well with Excite might create a weird opening page for your visitors, with all the keywords packed into the first paragraph. For all that effort and clunkiness, the site might still be listed low on Excite, show up in the wrong part of Infoseek, and never make the cut at Yahoo.

Well, you might be thinking, this isn't much of a primer on improving my site's ranking. That's exactly my point. There is not much you can do to improve your site's ranking aside from making it the best or only place to get information people need or want in a certain topic area.

The richest content sites on the Web can't possibly capture their whole essence in a title and one paragraph. Look at top Internet magazines like *Salon* at **www.salon.com** and ask how to capture their editorial focus in a list of keywords and a paragraph. You can't. They employ teams of writers tackling a variety of subjects from all angles. There's no single description aside from "magazine" that does the site justice. Here's *Salon*'s abstract at Yahoo:

> Salon—magazine of books, arts and ideas dedicated to the power of the written word.

That's it. There's no hype or list of buzzwords repeated over and over to trick people into visiting the site. If you want a contemporary magazine, go to *Salon*. If not, move on. The magazine is so thorough in its refusal to hype that it doesn't even list keywords in its meta tags aside from "Salon Magazine."

The key to *Salon*'s success isn't a gimmick that gets it listed at the top of a search on magazines. It's that the site is bursting with excellent articles and reviews that you won't find anywhere else. You'll see it referenced at other sites, hear it mentioned by colleagues, and possibly even receive an article sent around by e-mail. Outstanding material gets noticed.

**Outstanding Sites Will Get Noticed**

You will not, of course, be able to produce on your own a site with enough content to rival *Salon*. You might not even have a site that focuses on editorial content at all, but perhaps just sells your products. In that case, being found when people are looking for those products is important, and for that you should use the meta tags with keywords and an accurate description that you developed earlier in this section.

Your list of keywords can get extensive. The Allison's Cookies site, for example, uses more than fifty keywords in its meta tags to get anybody even remotely interested in all-natural cookies. Turn the page, and have a look.

<META NAME="keywords" CONTENT="vegan, cookie, vegan cookies, vegetarian cookies, vegan brownies, delicious, scrumptious, the best, wheat-free, chocolate, brownies, mint, chocolate chip, organic, baked goods, natural, mail order, gifts, no egg, no dairy, dairy-free, no animal products, healthy, unrefined, dessert, whole foods, allergy, hand-made, unrefined sugar, yummy, whole wheat, pastry, whole grain, gourmet, bakery, gourmet desserts, wheat-free cookies, kids, soy, lecithin, wheat-allergy, gluten-free, health, fitness, children, health-food, carob chip, date, bars, pecan, sucanat, chocolate-free, no cholesterol, low saturated fat, natural junk-food, maple syrup, honey, tofu, non-hydrogenated oil, oats, fudge, cardamom, coconut, lavender, lemon, mint, cinnamon, snickerdoodles, spice, flavorful, chewy, heavenly, tastes good, delightful, nutrition, nutritious, heart, blood pressure, hypertension, hyperactive, good, weight-loss, diets, health, light, wholesome, no TFAs, light, sunflower oil, hi-oleic">

You probably didn't know there were that many ways to describe a natural cookie! Does this extensive list of keywords guarantee that anybody searching on "vegan cookies" will find Allison's Cookies? No, but it helps. Using that search term on Excite found Allison's Cookies at number five, on Infoseek at number eighteen, and on Lycos at number four. However, the term "cookie" by itself didn't find Allison's in the top fifty at any of the sites. As with so many online businesses, occupying a niche is important. Lots of companies sell cookies, but only a handful of companies sell vegan cookies.

No matter how much Allison's Cookies sends notes to the search engines and uses the word *cookie* in the first part of the website and in the title, there's little chance the site will ever be near the top of a search on "cookie." There are too many other sites competing for that location. No amount of keyword tweaking and site manipulation will overcome that fact.

However, it never hurts to see what your competition is doing to outrank you. Visit **www.keywordcount.com** to see your site and a competitor's side by side. The free service goes to both homepages and lists the top ten words appearing on each, the meta tag keywords, and the meta tag description. Look over the results and see if you can make a few changes to improve your results.

After you've fine-tuned your site, go to **www.rankthis.com** and **www.positionagent.com** to run a free check of where your site is ranked at each search engine when people use a keyword or phrase that you specify.

Finally, to keep tabs on the latest search engine ranking methods, bookmark **www.searchenginewatch.com** and visit periodically. In addition to a set of tips for getting yourself properly listed, it watches which engines are doing what and passes the info along to you.

## Strategies to Avoid

There are a handful of strategies that you should avoid because they are misleading to the public and degrade the value of search engines for everybody.

- Do not use meta tag keywords that are irrelevant to your site in the hopes that people will accidentally find your site and like it so much that they will stay. People have tried this with the most commonly used search terms, most of which are pornographic or financial. Love and money run the world, but not everybody searching for them online is going to appreciate running into your stamp collecting page. Don't use *sex* and *money* as keywords unless your site does indeed pertain to sex and money.

- Do not repeat your keywords over and over in an attempt to make search engines think your page is the most important one on that topic. For instance, you might be tempted to repeat *stamps* thirty times in the meta tag of your stamp collecting site once you learned that *sex* and *money* were off-limits. One use of *stamps* is enough. Using it more than that is such a trite way to weasel a site higher in the rankings that most spiders watch for it. If you're found repeating keywords, some engines will refuse to list you at all.

- Do not try to get around the repeated meta tag restriction by repeating keywords on your homepage. For example, you might type the word *stamps* in the same color as your home-page background and paste it hundreds of times. Your visitors won't see it, but the search engines will see *stamps* so many times that they will think your site is more important to stamps than a post office. Wrong. The search engines are onto this one, too, and will ban your site for trying to trick them.

- Do not submit your site repeatedly to the same search engines in an attempt to overwhelm them into listing you in the top ten. A resubmission is fine if you disappear from the search engines or need to update your listing, but not if you're just trying to improve your ranking. Here again, the search engines will see what you're up to and ban your site.

Let me return to the theme of the last section, quality, for a dose of common sense. The search engines want to provide their visitors with the sites those visitors want to find. The engines are not interested in foisting your business off on anybody who ever stops by. Tools like meta tags and keywords are intended to help the search engines put your site in front of people who want to see the best sites on topics that interest them. If visitors come to expect nothing but junk results from a search engine, they'll stop visiting. That will destroy the engine. The engines know that and will do everything in their power to protect the integrity of their results from unethical promotion strategies.

Just remember that and you'll understand the spirit of search engine ranking. Build a top-notch site, then honestly present it to the world. When people look for sites of that type and find yours, they'll appreciate it, and the search engines will be happy to have provided the referral.

## Encourage Word-of-Mouth Marketing

Word-of-mouth is one of the best-known forms of marketing. I like your site, tell somebody, they like it and tell somebody else, and so on. Every business benefits from word-of-mouth marketing whether it exists online or not.

The difference is that it works faster and on a bigger scale for online businesses. Telling my neighbor about your flower shop on the corner requires that I go to his house, knock on the door, speak to him, and mention it. I probably wouldn't even think to recommend the flower shop unless my neighbor asked me over the fence one day if I knew of a good flower shop. The chances of my ever recommending your shop are low, and even if I did recommend it, I would only be doing so to one other person.

Online, however, it's a different story. If I read an excellent article about new potting soil at your flower site, I might want to forward that article to everybody I know who is interested in flowers. I can either send the entire article, send a link to the article, or just mention the site in an e-mail. In seconds, the note will be in the readers of several or even dozens of people. I have prescreened them myself by restricting the recipients to people I know are interested in flowers. The list of recipients will then visit your website, hopefully like it, bookmark it, and tell an even larger circle of friends. It can happen almost instantaneously online, whereas it takes time in the real world.

Although people will naturally recommend sites that they enjoy, you should provide some encouragement to do so. Some content-rich sites add a button to every article that says "E-mail this to a friend." You can do the same thing, although the programming is complicated if you want to customize the button to each page of your site.

A simpler way is to create a page that tells visitors how they can send anything they like to friends. Title it something like "Pass the Word" and provide general instructions. Most people will already know how to forward information of interest to them, but your page will help those who don't and will remind the ones who do of how easy it is. You can add a link to your "Pass the Word" page anywhere there's room on your site. A simple text link would be fine because it's a fine-print kind of feature.

**Encourage People to Pass the Word**

On the next page there's sample text that you could use on the "Pass the Word" page of your flower site:

> Thanks for stopping by www.myflowers.com! If you like something you read here, please feel free to pass it along to a friend. You can do so by copying the address from your browser window and pasting it into an e-mail note. One click on the link and your friend will be reading about begonias in no time. It'll take you all of ten seconds to show the path to floral bliss.
>
> Know somebody looking for a hobby? Show them our **annuals** section.
>
> Heard somebody complaining about yard work? Point them to our **low-maintenance flowers** section.
>
> Got a friend who's feeling down? They might like some **fragrant flowers**.
>
> There's something for everybody here. Thanks again for stopping by!

This is generic, of course. You should snazz it up a bit and make it more specific to your site by mentioning real links that might be of interest to your audience. You'll know your audience better than anybody, so point out a few ways that people they know can benefit from your site.

Once you've shown people how to forward specific information to their friends, why not give them an automated way to recommend your entire site? That very service exists at **www.recommend-it.com**. You enter your site information and are given code that you drop anywhere on your site, just like the affiliate programs. When a visitor clicks the button or text link that says "Recommend It," they are taken to a page maintained by Recommend-It that guides them through endorsing your site to a friend. After they recommend it, the service displays a link back to your site.

## Keep Visitors Coming Back

Most companies derive a huge part of their income from repeat business. It's cheaper to keep selling to an existing customer than it is to advertise for a new one. It's the same online. When people overcome the astronomical odds of ever finding your site among the millions out there, you should make sure they keep returning. That means fresh content, of course. But everybody has fresh content. What can you do that will make your site stand out? Several things, actually.

## Make Your Site Their Homepage

The ultimate coup is to become a user's browser homepage. That means that every time they fire up their browser, the first site they see is yours. Most people choose a search engine or news site or weather page, but if you can succeed in becoming so good in a niche that people want to start every Internet session with you, you're onto something big.

To encourage that, add a page that tells people how to make your site their homepage. Like your "Pass the Word" page, this one is just a set of instructions explaining how to make your page the first one they see. Here's an excerpt from my site:

> MICROSOFT INTERNET EXPLORER 4
>
> To make this your homepage, follow these simple steps:
>
> > From the View menu at the top of your screen, choose Internet Options.
> >
> > Click the General tab and change your homepage address to **http://www.jasonkelly.com**
> >
> > Click OK.
>
> The homepage will now be the first page you see when you launch your browser.
>
> NETSCAPE NAVIGATOR 4
>
> To make this your homepage, follow these simple steps:
>
> > From the Edit menu at the top of your screen, choose Preferences.
> >
> > In the left-hand Category list, click Navigator.
> >
> > Under "Navigator starts with," select "Homepage."
> >
> > Type: **http://www.jasonkelly.com** in the "Home page location" text field.
> >
> > Click OK.
>
> The homepage will now be the first page you see when you launch your browser.

On your actual page, you would offer instructions for additional versions of each browser and change my address to yours. Actually, leave my address there. That way all of your visitors will enter my site as their homepage. Thanks!

After creating your page, add a text link to at least your top page and possibly to every page of your site. It should just say "Make This Your Homepage" or something similarly witty.

## Offer an E-mail Newsletter

An e-mail newsletter is an excellent free service to keep people interested in what you're doing. It should be plain text with links to additional information at your website. One of the best I've seen is from *SmartMoney* magazine at **www.smartmoney.com**, a site for investors.

Once per week, *SmartMoney* e-mails a collection of its best new articles and features. Subscribers read a summary of the material and then have the option of clicking a link to the entire piece at the *SmartMoney* site. Here's an excerpt:

> SPECIAL OFFER
>
> ---------------------------------------------------------------------------
>
> Subscribe to SmartMoney magazine and receive up to 61% off the cover price. Click **here** to learn more.
>
> ===========================================================
>
> TOP STORY
>
> ---------------------------------------------------------------------------
>
> NASDAQ EXTENDS WEEK'S REBOUND
> Blue chips succumbed to profit-taking Friday, but the Nasdaq market continued its strong recovery from Monday's sell-off, briefly reaching a new high.
> **http://www.smartmoney.com/smt/markets/bulletin/**
>
> ===========================================================
>
> THE WEEK AHEAD
>
> ---------------------------------------------------------------------------
>
> SMALL STOCK SHINE
> Could it finally be time for small caps? They are indeed making a bit of a comeback. Here are some picks from two fund managers. Plus, everything you need to know to get ready for next week's market.

**http://www.smartmoney.com/smt/markets/news/index.cfm?story=199904234**

---

DAILY SCREENS

---

OH, BUILD ME A HOME
**http://www.smartmoney.com/smt/screen/index.cfm?story=19990423intro**

---

THE STOCK THAT FELL TO EARTH
**http://www.smartmoney.com/smt/screen/index.cfm?story=19990422intro**

---

MUTUAL FUND NEWS

---

FUNDS FOR THE JAPANESE RECOVERY
**http://www.smartmoney.com/smt/funds/index.cfm?story=199904191**

---

TECH FUNDS VALUE SHOP (SO TO SPEAK)
**http://www.smartmoney.com/smt/markets/funds/index.cfm?story=199904201**

---

EDITOR'S CHOICE

---

CISCO'S BUYING SPREE
Through home-grown technology and acquisitions, the networking giant is trying to be the supplier of choice when Internet telephony takes off. What's next on the shopping list?
**http://www.smartmoney.com/smt/stocks/index.cfm?story=199904231**

---

IS THERE LIFE AFTER VIAGRA?
News that sales of its blockbuster impotence drug have slowed has taken the air out of Pfizer stock. Looks like hype works in both directions.
**http://www.smartmoney.com/smt/stocks/index.cfm?story=199904211**

Quite an action-packed weekly, wouldn't you say? And this is only about half of it. *SmartMoney* also offers a daily newsletter for free. Each of the links after the teaser text takes readers to the *SmartMoney* site where they will have the opportunity to subscribe to the magazine and provide advertising revenue to the site. It's valuable to newsletter recipients and also valuable to *SmartMoney*.

By the way, notice that *SmartMoney*'s newsletter begins with an ad for a subscription? There's no reason you can't drop in one of your products at the top and bottom of your e-mail newsletters too. That way you'll offer readers the opportunity to purchase something directly from the e-mail and several other enticements to your whole site. Be discreet, but make your products known.

You can manage your e-mail newsletter list yourself by having people send you their addresses, then adding those to a distribution list in your e-mail program. However, this method can become a lot of work as your list grows.

**Let People Manage Their Own Accounts**

Instead, go to **www.listbot.com** and sign up for free mailing list management. The service enables you to ask demographic questions about your visitors, archive your messages, and create lists of unlimited size. Everything is managed from the website, so you never need to download software. Best of all, your subscribers manage their own accounts. That way, if some of their information changes they can update their profiles without ever needing to tell you. Your e-mail will automatically go to the new address.

Sending a note to your subscribers is a snap. You create a list ID, such as "Flowers." To send a note to everybody subscribed to the list, you would compose it in your e-mail program and send it to flowers@listbot.com. Everybody who subscribed receives the note.

The service is free because the e-mail you send to people will include ads placed by ListBot. They're small ads that won't delay the delivery of e-mail, but they're ads nonetheless and you can't control their content. If you would like the benefits of ListBot without the ads, you can sign up for ListBot Gold and pay $99 per year.

An alternative to ListBot is **www.onelist.com**, a similar service that offers additional customization features. Check out both services and choose the one that's best for you.

## Inform People of New Content

Static sites are called "cobwebs," and nobody likes them. If you're going to keep adding fresh content to your site, you should let people know that it's there. You can always send notification in your e-mail newsletter—which is the best way to announce all-new features—but there's a simpler way for people to learn about smaller additions.

It's called Mind-It and it's offered at **www.netmind.com**. Mind-It is free to users. They enter their e-mail address, then visit the site they want to monitor for changes. Once there, they specify what the service should watch. Users can be informed of any change, changes to specific text, graphic changes, link changes, and even the appearance of keywords that they specify. Whenever a change is detected, the user receives an e-mail alert with a link back to the page that's monitored.

When you add a Mind-It button on your site, people just click it and your address is automatically filled in for tracking. They choose their preferences and they're done. They will now be informed of any changes you make to that page. Note that you can put the form anywhere on your site, not just the top page. If you put it three levels from the top, that's the page that will be monitored for change. Some people put the form on every page of their site, some at the top of subsections, and some only on the top page. Choose which method you want and grab the code. Drop it in place and you've got another hook that will keep people coming back for more.

## Use Content Off Your Website

Relatively few people in the world will ever see your website. You've spent countless hours writing material or getting others to write it. There's a chance that when you post it to your website, only a handful of people will see it. That's a shame. You should get your best material out to the public for two reasons. First, because people will benefit by reading it and, second, because if they like what they read they'll visit your site.

## Contribute to Online Discussion Forums

The simplest way to magnify content past your site is to participate in online discussions. You read about discussion groups on pages 27–29, and the examples there show the right and wrong ways to approach them. You don't want to flagrantly hype your site to people who expect a meaningful discussion with like-minded folks. You'll be barraged by acid e-mail and lose all credibility in the very community you hoped to entice to your site.

Instead, genuinely participate. Just as there is no way to trick people into liking your site, there is no way to trick them into liking what you have to say. Either you pay attention to the information they're seeking and do a little work in providing it for them, or you throw any sort of comment out and sign it with your name and URL, hoping a few of the people will click over. For long-term success, go the first route. It's the only way to get people you really want coming to your site again and again. Others will just be clicking out of curiosity and will probably never return because there's no hook to make your site stand out.

The experience you want to create for people goes something like this: I am getting married, and I want to surprise my new wife with a special honeymoon that she'll never forget. However, I don't have much money. Is there anybody out there who can suggest affordable honeymoon destinations that don't seem cheap?

To find out, I search for honeymoons and end up in the message board at **honeymoons.about.com**. I don't see anything that says, "Hurry! Round-trip airfare and lodging to Turtle Beach Resort on Barbados only $800 per person! Going fast! Call 1-800-339-5671 or visit www.neatmoney.com!" Anything like that would instantly turn me off because there's no information. I can find vacation ads in my newspaper anytime. I want more than that.

Luckily, I find it under the heading "Santa Barbara is very romantic." Look at the difference in tone between the blatant ad and these two paragraphs:

> I love exotic, tropical places, but if the pocketbook just can't handle the plane fare to the other side of the world, I'd go to beautiful Santa Barbara for my honeymoon. It's my home town and I love it. It's semi-tropical with great weather most of the year.
>
> Although SB certainly is not a cheap place to visit, you can really do a lot in this small "city." There's the beach, shopping, sailing, a visit to the nearby channel islands, great hiking, wine tasting in the Santa Ynez valley, and lots of history and architecture in this old Spanish town. Of course, you can always brush elbows with the rich and famous.

At the bottom of the posting is a URL, **www.tropi-ties.com**. I click to find more good information like this and am greeted by a place to buy hats, bikinis, sandals, and almost everything else I will need for my beach vacation. That's how posting to discussion groups should be done. I gained valuable information about honeymooning in Santa Barbara and I also found a good place to get cheap vacation products. Never did I resent the link to Tropi-Ties.

I also found a helpful posting that suggested honeymooners should read the many articles at **www.theknot.com**. As far as I could tell, the person posting had no affiliation to The Knot. She had simply stopped by there for help planning her honeymoon and found it very helpful. So, she was passing her resource along to others. I went to The Knot and agreed with her that it's an excellent site, at which point I mentioned it to a friend of mine who recently got engaged.

Word-of-mouth marketing really works. Make your site excellent so that people appreciate it and tell others. Then go to the discussion groups where your target audience gathers and contribute valuable information.

## Let Other Sites Show Your Content

Some of those articles at The Knot are available elsewhere, most notably Yahoo. Allowing others to redisplay your best material is a simple way to give your site exposure to new visitors.

A great information distribution site is at **www.ramius.net**. Members contribute most of the information through discussion boards, but the site also redisplays articles from other sites. The presentation of your material at Ramius Network is top-notch, so you'll be proud to see your content and links to your site. The information is grouped into Yahoo-like categories for easy retrieval, and there's also a speedy search feature. You can contact Ramius Network about including your material by visiting the site or e-mailing information@ramius.net.

If you want others to read your material and you'd like to make money for your efforts, check out **www.isyndicate.com**. The company works with more than 70,000 websites to provide content. Some of that content can be yours whether you write articles, draw cartoons, or design software. iSyndicate offers several different programs for you.

Self-syndication is intended for small sites or one-person operations. As a self-syndicated content member, you will have your material distributed to interested websites with a link back to an archive site of your material hosted by iSyndicate. The company sells advertising on your archive site and shares the revenue with you.

The Content Licensor program works similarly except that your original material is licensed to interested sites for a fee that iSyndicate shares with you. The material is still archived with ad revenues, so there are two ways to make money in this program.

Notice that neither of these programs are intended to drive traffic to your site. Instead, they concentrate on making money for you directly off the content you create. However, your content can still drive traffic to your site by concluding each article with a link to your URL.

If you want to focus on increased traffic, iSyndicate has three ways to do so. The Express Site program puts your content on other sites and then charges you for any click-throughs back to your site. This could get expensive in a hurry, so be careful.

People might click to read your entire article, then go back to where they started. Their visit cost you money, and you didn't sell them anything. A better option is the Network Site plan, where your material is licensed to other sites. You make money off the licensing fee and you also increase the awareness of your site.

A third choice is the Community Site program. Your content is distributed to popular community sites like GeoCities and The-Globe.com. Members can then use excerpts from your material on their personal homepages and even have it updated automatically as you submit new content. The complete content is stored on co-branded pages at the community site. Lots of advertising happens there, and the money is shared between you, the community site, and iSyndicate.

As you can see, the options at iSyndicate are varied. I suggest that you visit the site, poke around a bit, and see where your plans best merge with their offerings.

## Publish Articles Offline

Because the Web is so competitive, sometimes the best way to promote your site is off the Internet. Many of my favorite sites came to me through newspaper stories, magazine articles, and newsletters. Getting your site into traditional publications is a tried-and-true marketing strategy.

If you produce a lot of content for your website, then you are in perfect position to produce it for other publications. Articles that work online will work offline as well. Simply find the magazines that relate to your topic area and query them to publish your articles. Two good places to find contact information for magazines are the *Writer's Guide to Magazine Editors and Publishers* published by Prima and the annual *Writer's Market* published by Writer's Digest Books. Find appropriate magazines and start mailing. Be sure to include your website address in your bio.

**Paper Articles Will Get Your Site Noticed**

Publishing articles in magazines is a career in itself called freelance writing. That may not be what you had in mind when you started your website. You might not enjoy writing, might not be any good at it, or just might be too busy to put words on paper several times a week. If that's the case, consider showing your website to other writers so that they can mention it. As you read your favorite trade and business magazines, pay attention to who writes the good stuff about your topic. Contact those writers with a complimentary letter and introduce your website to them. Not only are writers always looking for fresh material to write about, they enjoy recommending resources that they've found helpful. Just look at how many websites I've pointed out to you in this book. Every one of them benefits by being mentioned here. You might even become a customer of theirs all because you read about the various sites here. You too want to benefit by getting mentioned in print. If you can't write the material yourself, then go to the people who are writing it.

Finally, don't neglect the trusty letter to the editor. Anybody can get into print by writing a quick opinion piece on any newsworthy issue and firing it off to the local newspaper editor. Sign with your name and URL and you'll pick up a few extra visitors. If your topic has a universal appeal, consider writing to other newspapers as well. You can find a listing of every newspaper in the country at your local library's reference desk.

## Seek Reciprocal Relationships

Beyond professional content-sharing sites, don't forget to seek your own reciprocal relationships with sites that share your audience. The simplest ones to approach are information-only sites that will be happy to provide their visitors with a link to your site if it fits their topic area. They will probably agree to redisplay some of your content as well. As a website manager yourself, you know how hard it can be to come up with fresh content on a regular basis. If your site is about hot-air ballooning and you write a new article every Monday, you can be sure that other hot-air ballooning sites would like to show that article to their visitors, along with a link to your site.

Even competing commerce sites are surprisingly open to complementary relationships. If your hot-air balloon site sells products for balloons but nothing in the parachuting category, would it bother you to point skydivers to your favorite online parachute shop? Of course not. You don't sell those products anyway, and it's a great service to point your skydiving visitors to an equipment source. The online parachute shop won't mind returning the favor by pointing its hot-air ballooning enthusiasts back to you.

To find sites that target the same audience as you, search Yahoo for the category that contains your site. Visit the sites listed with yours to see if there are any good fits. If there aren't, expand your search by asking yourself how people interested in your site would conduct their own search. Type in those queries and see what comes up. Visit the sites for any good fits. If you still don't see any, that might be good because it means you don't have many competitors. As a final attempt, try searching About.com for your topic area. The human guides there do a good job of dredging relevant sites from the far corners of the Web. Don't forget to search on topics that are similar to yours but not the same, such as hot-air ballooning and parachuting.

Once you do find sites that match, e-mail the webmasters and ask if they'd be interested in a reciprocal relationship. It's important that you be specific in your note because webmasters are inundated with hundreds of solicitations every day. Their first instinct is to delete every note. Make yours stand out by being honest and showing exactly how you would like to cooperate with them. Here's a sample note:

> Dear Webmaster,
>
> I like your parachuting site very much. As the owner of a hot-air balloon site at **www.yoursite.com**, I have an interest in a similar audience. Perhaps we can share links back and forth between our sites to increase traffic and point our visitors to a site that would be closer to their interests.
>
> For my part, I would be happy to write about your site at my **related sites** page and even show sample products from your store at my **fun while flying** products page.
>
> In return, I would like to provide you with a few words about my site that you could display on your **balloon lovers** page. I can provide you with graphics and links to specific products of my own.

Finally, I can offer you hot-air ballooning articles from my **altitude essays** page and my **adventures in a basket** page. Both provide an insider's look at the sport of ballooning. In trade, I would like permission to show content from your site on my **other airborne observations** page. You would credit my material with a link back to my site, and I would do the same for yours.

I think we can make our respective sites more appealing to visitors by gathering helpful resources for airborne enthusiasts of all types. It would be a pleasure to create a relationship.

I look forward to hearing from you.

Sincerely,
Your Name

Notice the links that take the webmaster directly to the pages that you have in mind for reciprocal listings at your site, and the link that shows exactly where you would like to be listed at the partner site. That saves a lot of unnecessary back-and-forth e-mailing. The webmaster has enough information to make a decision and get back to you.

I have found that notes like this almost always result in an agreement. Why wouldn't they? Everybody benefits, and it doesn't require much work from either party. Links are links. The more pages that point to your site, the more traffic you'll receive. Other webmasters know this, of course, so they'll be open to a tradeoff, particularly in this case since you came to them. They didn't even need to approach you for the reciprocal relationship.

**Lots of Sites Will Work with You**

Which brings me to the final point. Be open to working with others who approach you. There's a good chance you'll receive a note like the one I show above. If the site that's proposing a relationship fits your standards, work with it. The energetic webmaster just saved you a lot of time spent finding and approaching their site for the same relationship. It came to you, so snap it up!

# Print Your URL Everywhere

When you have a website you're proud of, print the URL everywhere! It should be on your business cards, letterhead, signs, pens, coffee mugs, and so on. Anything you produce to promote your business should include a display of your website URL.

Unless the address itself is compelling enough to make people want to visit, put some teaser copy nearby so that people will want to know more. Grab something specific from your site. For instance, "Why do husbands cheat? Find out at www.yoursite.com" or "Two hundred women and a bottle of hooch! It's all happening at www.yoursite.com" or "www.yoursite.com, where SCUBA divers go when they're not wet."

Teaser copy like this will get people interested in visiting your site. Make sure that the teaser matches what they'll find when they actually arrive at your site. There's nothing worse than following up on the question of why husbands cheat only to discover that the site won't tell you.

While you don't need to be brash to get noticed, you should be interesting. For instance, I've seen sites that do in fact contain articles about marital infidelity. They were promoted with copy like "Your source for social articles." Now, who in the world is going to jump off a chair to visit that site? Nobody. Your copy needs to make people want to know more or arouse their curiosity. Social articles seem like homework, but "Lurk with other deviants at www.yoursite.com" seems like a worthwhile click.

Get creative. Think of your main editorial focus and pour some hot sauce on it. Look at it through a prism for better ways to say the same thing. Sure, your site is a collection of serious farming tips and techniques, but the best way to promote it is probably not by saying "A farming site." Instead, try "A mouse is the most important farm animal at www.yoursite.com."

# Garner Traditional Publicity

Your articles submitted to magazines and letters to the editor are traditional forms of publicity. Every business can benefit from them. Publicity is anything that puts you in the public eye without costing you anything. If it costs you money, it's advertising.

There are other forms of publicity beyond getting mentioned in print. If you can establish yourself as an expert on your site's topic area, you'll have a good chance of being called onto television and radio for your input. Think it can't happen to you? Think again. When a news story is hot, producers will turn to just about anybody for comment. If you've written a book, so much the better. But a website is nearly as good.

Take your hot-air balloon site, for instance. If a balloonist successfully navigates the Rocky Mountains during a fierce storm, the news is going to want experts to talk about the thrills and challenges of ballooning. Who better to offer an opinion than the owner of a ballooning website? Your local network affiliate station calls you in for a morning interview in which you come across as smooth and knowledgeable. Word gets out and before long you're talking on radio programs.

Your name creeps into the expert files on hot-air ballooning, outdoor recreation, and airborne sports. Before long, you're called onto a national program as the owner of www.yoursite.com, the leading hot-air balloon website.

You'll notice some interesting twists happening along the way. One producer doing a special on job-related stress calls you to see if ballooning is a good way to relieve stress. The call gives you an idea for a new angle: ballooning as an escape from today's fast-paced work environment. You create a new section on your site and begin submitting that angle to the media. Suddenly, you're a job-stress expert as well, still billed as the owner of www.yoursite.com.

This snowball effect happens all the time, and it brings gobs of attention. It doesn't happen easily, but it is certainly within your reach. To push it in the right direction, you'll need to get yourself and your website information in front of the right people. You do that with a media kit.

Your media kit should be an attractive folder containing a news release announcing the latest development at www.yoursite.com, your bio, a color printout of your homepage, a photo of you, and sample interview questions with your answers.

These are the basics. Get creative and add anything that will help your media kit glow with unique ties to your website.

Go to your library's reference desk and ask for a publication that lists TV and radio producers. There are several available. Scour the guide for programs that fit your topic area, and either write them down or photocopy the pages. Be sure that you get the station's phone number.

Return home and call each prospective producer. This step is vital because producers change jobs faster than ink dries. Your carefully prepared media kit sent with love to Amanda Farley will arrive on Hubert Mulcahey's desk and never get opened. Hubert wants nothing more than an excuse to get rid of his mail without ever opening it. Your misaddressed envelope is just the ticket.

**Present Your Site Only to People Who Are Interested**

Don't give Hubert the ticket. Call each producer to find out if the program still exists, get the name of the current producer at least until Friday, and then confirm the mailing address. Do not skip this step. A quick phone call can save you time spent preparing a media kit and the money it takes to produce the material and mail it.

Keep good records throughout this process, preferably in a database on your computer. You want to know whom you contacted when, what they said, and what your next action should be. That way, you can stay in touch with hot leads and become the expert that they rely on.

Once you've sent your initial media kit to hot leads, follow up a week later on the phone. Chat if they'll let you. You're trying to get a sense for how well they like your material and if they will want periodic updates. Tell them you'll send something now and again to get their reaction. Some will come right out and tell you to save yourself a stamp. Some will say that's fine but they'd prefer to receive it on the fax. Some will just say oh. Again, keep copious records.

After this initial stage of contacting, do keep in touch with the good ones by whichever method they indicate. If you fax, keep it to one page. If you e-mail, keep it short.

No matter how they tell you to stay in touch, you should occasionally send something through the regular mail. Faxes, e-mail, and voicemail are easy to ignore. They're also easy to deliver, which is why 10,000 of them arrive in a producer's life everyday. Mail costs money so fewer people use it. You should strategically mail something to your hot producers every six months or so.

One very good item is a Web Card. You first learned about Web Cards on page 89 as a potential affiliate program. They are full-color postcards of your website that you mail to potential clients or, in this case, media contacts. They're catchy and affordable. Visit **www.printing.com** to browse the various packages. One of these catchy cards with a handwritten note from you will keep your site in a producer's mind for some time. If one arrives every six months, you'll gradually become a trusted source.

Of course, all of this assumes you did your homework as explained and have narrowed your producers down to the ones who really do have an interest in what you have to say. Don't waste your money, your time, and their time with a mass mailing. Leave that to credit card companies and America Online. You want highly targeted contacts that will benefit by staying in touch with you. Such people will not resent your periodic mailings because they benefit from them. People who do not benefit will see your material as junk mail.

Another good way to get radio programs is to advertise in *Radio-TV Interview Report* from Bradley Communications. It's a magazine that comes out three times per month and is mailed to thousands of radio producers. You submit your information to Bradley, and they create an ad for you. Most of the advertisers are authors with books to sell, but your website can also be promoted well on radio. You can reach Bradley Communications at 800-989-1400.

Finally, if you do ever decide to blast a news release across the entire United States, don't do it yourself. You'll spend more money creating the materials and mailing them than if you just paid a public relations firm to handle it for you. Plus, journalists pay attention to news releases from PR firms, while they might not give yours a second glance.

A place to post your news releases online for free is at

**www.prweb.com**. Your story won't get picked up by many mainstream journalists, however, because the site attracts material of questionable value. It is free, after all, and anybody with access to the Internet can post whatever they consider to be a news release.

If you are more interested in professional PR services, which charge a fee, consider going to **www.businesswire.com** and **www.prnewswire.com**. It'll cost you around $500 to distribute 400 words across the entire U.S. media circuit. If you did it yourself, the postage alone would run you more than $2,000.

## Win Design Contests

Winning a design contest is good for your self-esteem, but in most cases that's about all. A few years ago, awards were also good for building traffic. People would see your site listed among the winners and click over for a look. That's how it used to be, anyway, when the Web was new and people were curious to see what constituted award-winning design.

That's not the case anymore. Few visitors care about yet another list of what somebody else considers to be great sites. Even if visitors do care, there are so many lists with so many sites that it's not very distinguished to win an award anymore. This volume problem is exacerbated by unscrupulous sites that toss an award to everybody who submits their site. Why? Because the winners—everybody who applies—will display the award-giving site's logo that just happens to link back to the award-giving site. It's a sleazy way to fish for traffic.

Despite this unfortunate state of affairs, there are still a few awards worth winning. They are actually judged, and veteran Web users respect the findings. It adds a bit of prestige when you display an award logo from one of these sites on your homepage. Winning the Lycos stamp of approval carries a lot more weight than winning Hank's Happy Homepage award.

Among the best-known award sites are Lycos Top 5% at **point.lycos.com**, Too Cool at **www.toocool.com**, and USA Today Hot Sites at **www.usatoday.com**.

Even these sites and others of their ilk aren't worth a lot of effort. When was the last time you knew somebody who wanted to find information on the Web and decided to start their search with a list of award-winning pages? It doesn't happen because people want specific information from the Internet, not random coolness. Even Yahoo's surfer picks are little more than entertainment. Just because Websurfer Jane thinks the online feline page is the greatest thing she can do with her time doesn't mean that you'll agree.

I suggest that you rely on good design, good content, and good word-of-mouth marketing to make your site popular. The best award you can win is a ton of traffic.

# Place Banner Ads

By now you've seen thousands of banner ads. They appear at search engines and popular sites everywhere, blinking, enticing, and sometimes even making noises for you to click on them. When you do, you arrive at a new site or a promotional page selling you something. Banner ads are like billboards on the Internet.

You can join a free banner ad exchange service or pay to place banner ads pointing people to your site.

## Free Banner Ads

In a banner exchange program, you submit a banner that advertises your site. It will be displayed on a rotating basis at other sites. In exchange, you clear space on your site to display promotional banners from other participants in the program.

**Free Banners Might Not Fit with Your Site**

The worst part about free banner exchanges is that they tend to look unprofessional on your site. You have little control over which banners will appear on your pages, no control over their appearance, and you're forced to show a link to the banner exchange's homepage. That means everybody coming to your site will see that you're using free services to promote yourself and that they can also sign up for those free services. The most respected sites on the Internet do not use free services, so you may not want that scarlet letter right at the top of your homepage.

Some site owners swear by the free exchanges. They say that participation does indeed drive more people to their sites and that those people are somewhat prescreened because they responded to an ad that told them exactly what the site was about. Thus, if it was a woodcarving banner ad, then everybody clicking on it would be interested in woodcarving and should like the woodcarving site that arrives after clicking.

Ultimately, it's up to you. I personally think free ad services look, well, free. But if a low-budget look can succeed in doubling your traffic, then it might be worth it.

The most popular free banner ad service is the LinkExchange Banner Network at **adnetwork.linkexchange.com**. It's run by the same wholly owned subsidiary of Microsoft that runs ListBot. The service brings together more than 450,000 sites that collectively reach over 60 percent of the Web's traffic. For every two times that you display a banner on your site, you earn a credit to have your banner shown once on another site. You have limited control over what types of sites you are willing to advertise and the types of sites you want to have display your ad. Once you've registered and set up the necessary ad space on your site, you will be able to see daily and weekly traffic reports.

Other free banner exchange services are at the following sites: **www.bannerco-op.com**; **www.hyperbanner.net**; **www.hyperexchange.net**; **www.intelliclicks.com**; **www.massivetraffic.com**; and **www.rapidlinks.com**.

## Paid Banner Ads

Paid banner advertising can be very expensive. You're entering the realm of ad agencies that have brought traditional rate schedules from magazines, billboards, and airport lounges to the Internet. You've been forewarned. Don't be seduced by the large numbers of people who will be seeing your ads. It's easy for ad services to say that your banner will be seen by more than

20 million Web visitors. If none of them click, who cares? Even if they all click over to your site, what if none of them buy anything? Expensive advertising is risky.

## Don't Be Seduced by Big Numbers

I know firsthand that the seduction of big numbers is powerful. I once placed an advertisement in a national newspaper with a circulation of more than 18 million readers. I figured that if only one percent of the readers looked at my ad, that would be 180,000 people. If only one percent of those purchased my product, that would be 1,800 sales. I would clear $10 per sale. Wow! My head spun as I thought about the $18,000 of easy money on the way.

Guess how many people responded to the ad? One. Even worse, he only wanted information. So for the money I spent to put my product in front of 18 million readers, I had one phone call, which was an inquiry.

Be very wary of advertising. Anybody can toss out huge numbers of consumers who will be exposed to your ad. So what. There are 280 million people in the country. Most of them don't care what you're doing or what you're selling. Advertising to the overwhelming majority is a waste of money.

## Target Your Audience and Pay for Results

You want to target specific audiences and, if possible, you want to pay only when people seeing your ad actually click over to your site. This is called, appropriately enough, pay-per-click. Few sites or advertising networks offer it because they argue that there is value in having people see your banner ad whether they click it or not. That may be true for Coca-Cola, Ford, and IBM who are building long-term brand awareness. I doubt very much that your website is going to build long-term brand awareness to rival such companies. The only brand awareness you're looking for is to be bookmarked and regularly visited by a relative handful of Web users. You are not creating an ad campaign the way corporations do, you're seeking a few extra visitors. You want to pay only for results.

Finding such an arrangement will be difficult, however. Advertising sites don't have any control over your banner ads and their ability to generate clicks. If you give them a crummy ad and nobody clicks it, they didn't make a dime for their efforts and they lost the opportunity to host a different ad that would have made money for them. Few advertising sites or services are eager to enter that type of business arrangement.

## How You Will Be Charged

If you can't find a pay-per-click deal, start looking at what you'll get for your money. How specific will your audience be? If you started a travel essay page, you should only advertise on travel sites. Remember my one phone call out of 18 million readers. That ad failed because the 18 million readers weren't interested in my product. It would have been far better to advertise to 1,800 readers who have an interest in what I was selling. It's the same for you. Don't pay for 50 million general Web users to see your travel essay ad. Pay for 5,000 avid travelers to see it.

Ask what volume of impressions you can expect. An impression happens when one entire page of text and graphics loads onto a visitor's browser. That page will include your ad. Every time an impression of your ad occurs, it's assumed that the visitor saw your ad. You will usually be charged by the CPM, which stands for cost per thousand impressions. The amount can be anything, but is usually under $100 and sometimes less than $1.

You judge the effectiveness of your banner ads by the click-through rate, or CTR. That's the percentage of impressions that result in a click on your banner. A good CTR is anything above 2 percent. If you pay a $1 CPM and achieve a 2 percent CTR, you would be getting 20 visitors for each $1 you spend. That's a cost per click of 5 cents, which is quite good. Most people pay between 10 cents and $1.00 per click. They either pay a higher CPM or achieve a lower click-through rate.

## Where to Advertise

Any of the big search engines will sell banner ad space to you. The most popular method is the keyword trigger where your site on diving is advertised every time somebody searches on "diving." Recently, Yahoo charged $1,000 per month per word and guaranteed 10,000 impressions. Thus, the worst you would achieve is a CPM of $100, which is 10 cents per impression. You wouldn't know the click-through rate or cost per click until the month was over.

There are hundreds of online advertising agencies that maintain ad networks. One of the biggest is at **www.doubleclick.net**. The DoubleClick network amasses the Web's most popular destinations into ten user interest categories. The global network reaches 48 million users per month on 350 sites, but you can also target locations by area code, city, state, and region. The DoubleClick Direct program offers a pay-per-action fee schedule where you are only charged when people click to your site, enter lead information, or download some type of product sample.

Another company worth checking out is at **www.flycast.com**. It specializes in surplus advertising space, which is the 75 percent of all banner ad slots that go unsold each day. Sites with excess banner ad inventory are eager to make some money off their slots, so they will negotiate lower CPM rates with Flycast. Supposedly, that savings is passed along to you. The Flycast network reaches more than 22 million people a month.

Adsmart at **www.adsmart.net** will take your banners to specific sites that the company has divided into several tiers based on popularity. Among the marquee sites are Better Homes and Gardens, National Geographic, and Standard & Poor's. The prices are expensive. You'll pay a $35 CPM at the National Geographic site, which gets 9 million impressions per month. You can also target your ads by content, keyword searches, or geographic region.

## Designing a Good Banner

Regardless of whether you are part of a free banner exchange or you've paid gobs of money to put your banner in front of millions, you always want to place good banners. People have tried everything from running contests to making the banner look like an official operating system error to insulting viewers. Out of this experimentation, a few successful strategies have emerged.

## Street-Tested Tips

The usual click-through rate on banner ads is 2 to 4 percent. That is an ad that loads quickly, appears in front of people who care about its product, and uses eye-catching colors.

Several studies have shown that animation raises the CTR of a banner ad to a 5 to 6 percent range. There appears to be little agreement as to what type of animation works best. Tiny, slowly moving elements in the banner ad will not attract as much attention as having the entire ad space change every second. However, an annoyingly animated ad will irritate people. The only general consensus is that something in your banner ad should move.

Even more powerful is a moving banner ad that is also interactive. That means it presents a pull-down list or a dialogue box that the visitor can actually manipulate directly within the ad. There's no need to go to the advertiser's site.

A good example of this technique is found in bookstore banner ads. Both Amazon.com and barnesandnoble.com have run ads that include a search box directly to their online stores. The ads show teaser text like "What books would your Dad like for Father's Day? Enter his hobby here." The user then enters a hobby like fly-fishing and is immediately taken to a results page of fly-fishing books with instructions on how to send them gift wrapped directly to a different address, presumably the dad's.

**Get Those Banners Clicked**

Such banner ads don't even seem like ads. Instead, they're like features on the website. In market research surveys, people have revealed that they didn't even know they were buying from a website different from the one they were visiting.

Interactive banner ads have achieved click-through rates of more than 20 percent. So, if there's a feature at your site that can draw people in through an input box or pulldown list, use it.

The possibilities are endless. If you have a model railroading site, your ad could say "Do you prefer steam or diesel?" Based on the response, you would take the visitor to your steam engine page or your diesel engine page. If you run a celebrity commentary page, your ad could say "Who's the sexiest woman alive?" A pulldown list could show the top actresses and models for users to choose from. They would then be taken to that woman's profile on your site.

Banner ad sales representatives from Yahoo spoke to a conference in New York and passed along a few additional design suggestions. Here they are:

- Any banner is good for only two weeks. After that, nobody notices.
- The words "Click Here!" will boost response dramatically.
- A text link below the ad that instructs people to click will increase response. For example, "Click here for America's best flower seeds."
- A sense of urgency seems to attract people. For example, "Final week!"

## Banner Design Tools

Before you design your banners, visit **www.bannertips.com** for the best collection of banner design tips on the Web. You may look over the long list of considerations and decide that you'd rather hire a professional. You'll find a list of them at Banner Tips.

To design your banners for free on the Web, visit **www.animation.com** and **www.quickbanner.com**. They offer several sizes and templates that you use to create just the right look for your site.

You can use any graphics software capable of saving files in a GIF or JPEG format to create your banner ads. Products from Adobe, Corel, Microsoft, and other publishers will do the job.

However, the consensus among most banner design professionals is that Macromedia's *Fireworks* is the best. It was designed from the start to create graphics for the Internet, so it has a slew of custom tools like browser previews, mouse rollover mapping, and clean HTML generation. It costs $200 and runs on both Macintosh and Windows. You can find out more at **www.macromedia.com/software/fireworks**.

# Visit Marketing Sites Regularly

The best information about marketing a website is available online. Because opportunities come and go so quickly, often the only medium fast enough to catch them is the Internet. These sites will keep you apprised of the latest developments.

- **The Web Marketing Information Center** from Wilson Internet Services is a huge collection of articles from hundreds of sites. You can search for a specific topic or browse the clickable index. Learn about analyzing site traffic, banner ad design, e-mail marketing, promotion, and sponsorships. There's also a free monthly e-mail newsletter called *Web Marketing Today* that will deliver useful tips right to your computer.
  **www.webmarketingtoday.com/webmarket**

- **forkinthehead.com** is a fun site by Cathie, Nick, and Dave. The weird name comes from their philosophy that flawed websites deserve a fork in the head. Cathie writes articles about promotion, Nick about online commerce, and Dave about website design. They also host guest articles from time to time.
  **www.forkinthehead.com**

- **NETrageous** is a Web marketing company that has gathered its favorite products and articles into one place for you. There are lots of plugs for their products throughout, but the products are relevant to marketing your site, and you just might find something worthwhile. The articles are good, too.
  **www.netrageousresults.com**

- **Sell It!** focuses on everything needed to succeed at e-commerce. A lot of the site explores the operational side of your business, like how to build a shopping cart and what kinds of products work best, but because marketing is critical to every site it covers that in detail as well. Much of it gets right to the point, such as a recent article entitled "Top Ten Tips for Creating a Successful E-commerce WebSite."
  **www.sellitontheweb.com**

• **Hits to Sales** brings together the best advice from ADNet International, a firm that helps companies create successful affiliate programs. Its articles are good because they include links to example sites that are doing everything right. Sometimes that's the best way to learn.
**www.hitstosales.com**

• **VirtualPROMOTE** makes its philosophy clear in its slogan, "Promote or Die." That says it all. The site is a comprehensive set of everything you need to get the word out. There are discussion forums, expert articles, recommended tools, link exchanges, and so on. The site is searchable and offers a popular e-mail newsletter called *VirtualPROMOTE Gazette*. I've subscribed to the gazette for years and find its marketing advice to be among the best available.
**www.virtualpromote.com**

• **WebPromote** is probably the most scholarly of the marketing sites. Its articles focus on industry evidence to find new trends. It uses surveys, interviews with consultants, and reports from the front lines of e-commerce to put ideas in your head. A recent guest expert on the site pointed out that banner advertising is not effective by itself. Sites must also use permission e-mail, such as the newsletter technique you learned about on page 75.
**www.webpromote.com**

• **Promotion World** has a tutorial that covers the basics quickly. All you do is press the NEXT button to push your way through lessons on search engines, meta tags, banner exchanges, and so on. The site also publishes articles and collects useful services from around the Web.
**www.promotionworld.com**

• **PromotingYourSite.com** purports to tell you what makes people click. It's easy to find reciprocal links at the site's message board, get free content for your e-mail newsletter, and read real-world advice from a pro.
**www.promotingyoursite.com**

# 8 Advertising on Your Site

When you have a site that's cooking along with steady traffic, you should consider accepting advertising. You'll make money and, if you choose advertisers carefully, your visitors will benefit from seeing products that they are interested in owning. The only ads people resent are the ones for products that don't interest them whatsoever.

## Deciding Whether to Accept Paid Advertising

You may feel that most advertising is annoying and that the deterioration of your site's pure image isn't worth the few extra bucks you'll make by running ads. If so, you're finished with this chapter.

However, if the editorial focus of your site lends itself to certain products, I think you're missing an opportunity to offer your visitors just what they're looking for—and get paid for doing it.

Picture this. You're interested in whitewater rafting so you hop on the Web and search for it. You find a rafting site with excellent articles. At the top of one article is a banner ad for a rafting company in the mountains near your home. You click on the ad and discover that the company is looking for part-time guides. Instead of just reading about rafting, you're now in position to get paid to learn about rafting. All of this came from a banner ad that the rafting company paid the rafting site to run.

When you think about it, banner ads are just glorified links to more information. Of course the company paying to place the banner ad wants people to click it because it hopes to get something—usually money—from the extra traffic. There's nothing wrong with that. As long as the product or service the company offers is congruent with the interest of your visitors, everybody benefits. People come to your site, see an ad for something they want, and click it. They're happy, the advertiser is happy, and you're happy because you were paid for running the banner.

Viewed in this way, advertising is not such an annoyance. I urge you to only advertise products and services that have a direct tie-in to the interest of your visitors. That means you need to know your editorial focus precisely so that you understand why people come to your site.

So your first consideration in deciding whether to accept paid advertising is whether there are any products or services that tie-in to your audience.

Next ask yourself if you want to invest the necessary time to run ads. You will need to contact prospective companies, pitch them on your focused audience, accept their ad, put it in rotation at your site, and collect the money. It's quite a bit of work.

## Deciding on the Types of Ads You'll Run

There are a lot more ways to advertise than the ubiquitous banner. It's the most common type of ad on the Internet, but other types can pull better response rates because they don't look like ads.

You'll probably run a combination of ad types on your site. Sometimes they work well together, as in a small button next to some textual information promoting a product or service. Read over the various types of ads, and give some thought to which type will fit best on your site.

## Text Link

My favorite online ad is the lowly text link. You'll recall from Chapter 5 that text links are a great way to push the products you sell as an affiliate. It works the same for companies advertising on your site because a text link is integrated with your material and is therefore perceived to be endorsed by you.

Which, by the way, it should be. You don't want to schlock products on your visitors that you would never dream of purchasing yourself. It makes your site look bad, and it's a lousy way to do business.

By choosing companies with products and services that you personally recommend, you'll put yourself in a good position to endorse them in your own words. That's the most effective form of advertising. Just listen to your favorite radio talk show host sometime. Notice that they read ads during breaks, in the middle of traffic reports, and before the weather? Those ads are the most expensive because the host's personal presentation makes them very effective. "Oh," listeners say to themselves. "Talking Tom gets his car washed at Central Suds. Maybe I should try it, too."

**Text Links Are Often the Best Choice**

It works the same way at your site. Instead of a banner ad, you could place a shaded box at the top of one of your articles that says this:

> Looking for a new home? Many of my friends have tried **Rapid Realty** and report that it's the fastest way to narrow your choices. The powerful search tool sifts through every home in your area matching your criteria. Each listing includes a photo that you can click to enlarge, complete info, and a phone number. To find your home, visit **Rapid Realty** or call 1-800-566-3496.

The same information could be contained in a banner ad that blinks photos of homes and quick headlines like "The most powerful home search on the Web." However, the personal endorsement of the text link approach is important to people. Notice that you didn't actually use Rapid Realty for your home, you simply reported that your friends found it helpful.

An additional benefit of using text links is that they load instantly. In several studies on banner ad effectiveness, a quick load time was determined to be more important than a flashy design. That makes sense. If people never even see the ad because it takes too long to load, it won't be very effective. With text links, load time is as quick as possible.

## Banners and Buttons

Banners and buttons are the most common forms of online advertising. People are used to seeing them, they know they're ads, and because of that many of them are ignored completely.

Not always, though. If a niche site runs banners for products that are solidly within that niche, people will look. Rafters want to go rafting and they want to buy river gear. Home buyers want to—here's a big surprise—buy homes. Products and services that will help them do that are of interest. Pet owners want to buy products that will make owning a pet more fun. Banners and buttons that advertise such products to interested people will get noticed.

Banners and buttons come in standard sizes, but you can make yours any size you want. The standard full banner size is 468 × 60 pixels and the full square button size is 125 × 125 pixels. Banners are usually at the top and bottom of pages while buttons are usually on the sides or within text.

I've had a lot of luck with odd sizes and unusual placement. For instance, banners that are smaller than the normal size seem to get noticed more. A good alternative size is the 230 × 32 pixel mini-banner used at the top pages of Yahoo and About.com. I also use that size at the top page of my site. There are two advantages to smaller banners. First, they take up less of your precious screen space. Second, they load quicker than big banners.

Going even smaller can create a solid impact. For instance, a tiny button used in conjunction with a text link paragraph creates a visual draw with all the benefits of the personal endorsement. The tiny button should be linked to the advertiser in case anybody clicks on it instead of the text link. Here's the same Rapid Realty text ad with a tiny home graphic included:

> Looking for a new home? Many of my friends have tried **Rapid Realty** and report that it's the fastest way to narrow your choices. The powerful search tool sifts through every home in your area matching your criteria. Each listing includes a photo that you can click to enlarge, complete info, and a phone number. To find your home, visit **Rapid Realty** or call 1-800-566-3496.

It's a simple touch, graphically appealing, and quick loading. Run on an appropriate realty site, I think this ad would perform well.

## Sponsorships

A sponsorship is the most serious commitment an advertiser can make to your site. It's a two-way endorsement where you are saying that you highly recommend the company and the company is saying that it respects your site. You charge more for a sponsorship than any other ads, and you would usually be required to grant exclusivity to the company for the duration of their sponsorship. It's bad form to have Coke sponsor your site and then run ads for Pepsi. If you do happen to get Coke to sponsor your site, please let me know how you did it.

Companies will usually want to sponsor a certain area of your site or an e-mail newsletter. For example, your real estate chat room or message board could be brought to your visitors by Rapid Realty. That message would appear all over the site section, and you would probably also include other ads to specific parts of the Rapid Realty site or to a new service the company is pushing.

Sponsorship of e-mail newsletters is growing in popularity because the audience has an even more proven interest than your typical site visitor. Somebody visiting a real estate site is probably interested in real estate. Somebody who has taken the time to subscribe to a real estate newsletter is definitely interested. Rapid Realty would like nothing more than to have its name and products placed at strategic locations in your next several issues.

### Avoid Pop-up Ads

When you visit some sites, a separate browser window opens on your screen and loads an advertisement. I can't imagine the complete lack of thought that went into devising this technique. Aside from music-playing animated icons, the pop-up ad is the most annoying Web gimmick in use. Everybody I surveyed in writing this book says they immediately close the extra browser session before the ad ever loads. The advertiser is wasting money and the site is angering its visitors.

So don't use pop-up ads unless you want to waste your advertiser's money and anger your site visitors.

## Run Your Advertisements Simply

The simplest way to run ads is by time of exposure. The advertiser pays you to place an ad on your site for a week. At the end of the week, you change the ad to the next paying advertiser, show your own ad, or give the current client some free time. You don't need to track click-throughs by setting up special links and internal promotion pages like those used by the search engines. You just drop the ad on your page for the specified period of time and collect the money.

### Prove Your Traffic

In order to attract clients to this type of arrangement, you will need to prove your level of traffic. Your hosting service or any of the tracking tools that you read about on pages 73–75 will be able to provide you with that information. When prospective advertisers know the editorial focus of your site and the number of visitors you receive, they'll be able to make an informed decision as to whether they should advertise.

Notice that advertisers are interested in the number of visitors you receive, not the number of hits. A hit happens whenever your browser loads a file from the Internet. A single page of your site might contain a text file, four graphic files, and the HTML that tells the browser how to display it all. That's six files in all. When somebody views that page, six hits are counted.

As you can see, hits are not visitors. A rule of thumb in the industry is that taking 13 percent of a site's hits will tell you the approximate number of visitors. This is not scientific by any means, but it's used by almost everybody. If you had 1,000 hits on Tuesday, your site was probably visited by 130 people.

Be prepared to talk page views and visitors to prospective advertisers. A page view occurs whenever an entire page with all of its graphics and text has loaded into a visitor's browser. Advertisers will want to know the number of people coming to your site and how many individual pages are being seen each month.

Don't be scared by any of this. You do not need to have Yahoo levels of traffic to be appealing to advertisers. Your lower rates combined with a highly targeted audience will make your site a viable option for lots of businesses. Remember that advertising to the whole world doesn't work. Companies know that, and they're always looking for ways to narrow the world down to their target customers. If your site delivers even a handful of those target customers, you're in the running to make some advertising money.

## Have Advertisers Track Their Own Click-throughs

Explain to advertisers that they will need to track the click-through success of their banners on their own. The usual way for them to do so is by establishing a special page at their site where people clicking on the banner arrive. A customized page is the best bet because it creates an integrated feel. For instance, if you clicked on that rafting company banner I mentioned earlier you might arrive at a page that began with "We're glad you saw us at The Rafting Connection, the best place for rafters online. Now, you're at the best place for rafters in the water!"

The page would be accessed only by people clicking on the banner from The Rafting Connection. That means anybody arriving there is a click-through and should be counted. After a few days, the rafting company will know what kind of success its banner ad at The Rafting Connection is achieving.

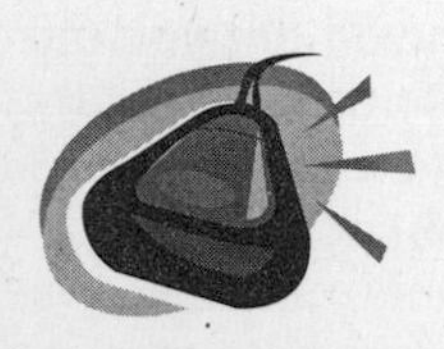

**Advertisers Should Track Their Own Click-throughs**

Notice that this setup relieves you of all tracking responsibilities, which is great news. Your only job is to place the banner and link it to the place requested by your client. This may not seem like such a big benefit to you at first, but it is.

I've heard horror stories from owners of small sites who tried tracking advertising click-throughs for their clients. One webmaster completely botched the job and showed the advertiser a success rate that was far higher than what actually happened. Unfortunately for the site, the advertiser also tracked the click-throughs and knew the real number. The advertiser concluded that the site owner was being dishonest and withdrew all future advertising.

Another site promised prospective advertising clients that it would be able to track click-throughs. Only after signing up several clients and collecting their money in advance did the owner learn that its hosting service would not allow tracking software to run on the server. The site could not afford its own server and the staff to run it, and so had to inform the new clients that it would not, in fact, be able to track click-throughs after all. No deal, the clients said. Untracked advertising is a waste of money. The site needed to refund the deposits and start gathering new clients that would track their own click-throughs.

Don't get caught in situations like these. In the first case, the client was tracking the ad anyway! The site never needed to fuss with its own tracking mechanism, yet its inability to deliver on the promise cost it a client.

You just deliver the high-quality site and loyal visitors to advertisers. Most will be able and willing to track their ads on their own.

If you have your own server and want to provide complete advertising packages to your clients, including tracking, multiple banners per account, statistics sliced every which way, and so on, then you'll need some help. Check out the services at **www.adforce.com** and **www.bondsmith.com**, and the software at **www.centralad.com**.

AdForce will do the work for you and charge by volume. Bondsmith manages your advertising load from its server and also charges by volume, starting at $5 per month for up to 5,000 impressions. Central Ad sells software for around $600 that you install once on your server.

## Seek Ongoing Advertisers

The ultimate coup in the advertising game is to amass a group of clients that continue advertising with your site every month. If possible, you should establish an automatic payment plan where you bill a credit card on the first of each month and run the client's ads continuously.

Like so many other parts of this business, a high-quality site will deliver this arrangement to you. If your site is the best in its class, people will continue visiting it on a regular basis. Those people will have common interests, and word will get out to others with the same interest. Your traffic will grow, especially if you give it a nudge with some of the marketing techniques you learned in Chapter 7. The growing traffic of like-minded people will provide steady business to advertisers who offer products and services squarely within your site's niche.

On the theme of keeping your advertising simple, this is the pinnacle. You will not need to seek new advertisers often if at all, and you will not need to invoice and follow up on collections. Instead, you simply run the ads on your site, updating them whenever the advertiser has a new ad or requests a new twist on your personal endorsement, and charge the credit cards each month.

You will achieve a steady cash flow directly into your bank account just by keeping your site at its best.

# Participating in Ad Networks

One way to get advertisers quickly is to participate in an ad network. You first learned about ad networks on page 148 in the section explaining that you can advertise your own website through an ad network. Now you're on the flip side of that coin. You can also accept advertising from those same ad networks.

## You Lose a Little Control . . .

The disadvantage is that you won't have much control over the products or services that get advertised on your site. You'll just drop in code from the ad network that allows whatever banners it's currently pushing to appear on your site. There's some amount of customization available to you but certainly not as much as you'd have choosing advertisers on your own.

Keep in mind that ad networks want to put the right products in front of your visitors as much as you do. They know that estate planning products won't sell on a site for children, therefore, they won't run estate planning ads there.

When you register your site with an ad network, you will describe your audience to the best of your knowledge. Often, a representative from the ad network will call to verify the information and will visit your site. They will build a site profile that is entered into the database for potential advertisers to examine. The advertisers will see what kinds of people visit your site and decide whether your audience is a good fit with their product or service.

So you can see that your site won't be thrown completely into left field with ads that don't interest any of your visitors. However, there will be times when ads targeting "general" audiences will show up on your site, and there will be occasions when an advertiser will get sloppy and accidentally put the wrong product or service on your site. If you don't mind seeing "general" ads for cars, vacations, holiday gifts, and other similar wide-ranging products, then you probably won't mind participating in an ad network.

## . . . But Make a Lot of Money

The disadvantage of losing some control over the ads that appear on your site can be offset by the advantage of making lots of money. There's not a whole lot you need to do once you join an advertising network aside from keeping your site appealing and the traffic levels high.

The ad network will find the ads for you and automatically serve them up to your site. The big networks will have little trouble keeping your inventory full of moneymaking ads. You will earn a commission that varies from 25 to 75 percent of the CPM rate that the ad network negotiates with the advertiser. You are usually paid within one week of when the network receives payment from the advertiser.

**Let the Experts Handle Your Advertising**

This is even easier than establishing an automatic pay system with clients that you choose. You never find clients, invoice them, or enter the fun world of collection (unless you sign up with an untrustworthy ad network that doesn't pay you). You just run your site and keep the ad network code in place so that the ads appear where they're supposed to be. Payment from the ad network comes in the mail or directly into your bank account.

## Whether to Grant an Exclusive

You will need to decide whether to grant a certain network exclusive rights to sell space on your site. If you do, then only your staff and the network can put ads on your site. You cannot also participate in other ad networks. You will earn more for exclusivity—sometimes up to an additional 20 percent commission—but you'll lose the business that might have come your way through other networks.

If the network you join is big enough, exclusivity shouldn't be a problem. The only sites that are ever hampered by exclusive arrangements are sites that have outgrown their network's capabilities. In those cases, the networks are usually eager to rise to the occasion or willing to renegotiate the contract.

## Requirements to Get In

The requirements for joining an ad network vary. Some of the biggest will not be available to you right away. For example, the DoubleClick Select exclusive requires your site to:

- Deliver one million impressions per month.
- Demonstrate current promotional and marketing programs that will produce additional traffic.
- Specialize in one of the current hot content categories. At the time of this writing, those categories were automotive, business and finance, entertainment, health, news, directories, sports, technology, and family.

It ain't easy getting into DoubleClick Select, but it's worth it if you can. Your site will be pitched to advertisers by a worldwide sales force of more than two hundred media representatives. Also, it gets around the loss of control disadvantage by providing you with complete authority to approve or disapprove of every ad being considered for display on your site. Sounds like heaven. Now, if it weren't for that pesky one million impressions per month requirement . . .

There's still hope for those of us snorkeling well below one million. Burst Media requires only 5,000 impressions per month and makes the reasonable request that you not make your online living as a porn purveyor. Burst doesn't maintain an ad network nearly as extensive as DoubleClick's but, then again, you don't run a site nearly as popular as *U.S. News & World Report*'s.

## Networks to Consider

When you are just beginning and don't have a lot of traffic, register at **www.ad-up.com**. The company allows sites of all popularity to join its network and even encourages highly specific sites with limited viewership. Individually, such sites are not appealing to advertisers. However, taken as a group, they can command enough traffic to get advertising dollars. Ad-Up is so committed to the little guy that it structures its commission payment schedule like an affiliate program. You won't receive your first monthly check until your earnings exceed $50.

Burst Media at **www.burstmedia.com** requires your site to show at least 5,000 impressions per month. It's a full-featured service that provides you with a control panel and up-to-the-minute statistics on your impressions and earnings. Go to the site's gallery of current members to see the varied sites you will be joining. It's a solid group of moderate-traffic sites.

If you have at least 100,000 impressions per month, check out Flycast at **www.flycast.com**. Its AdRegistry application forces advertisers to register their ads in specific categories. You can then block certain of these categories so that none of the ads in them are shown on your site unless you approve them on an individual basis. Visit its gallery of members—called "affiliates" here—and you'll notice an uptick in the professionalism as compared to some of the smaller networks. Websites like **www.carsmart.com** and **www.yack.com** are obviously not part-time ventures from somebody's kitchen table.

You're now arriving at the Internet's equivalent of Madison Avenue. These companies operate the largest ad networks, enforce the stiffest requirements, and make the most money for everybody involved. DoubleClick at **www.doubleclick.com** keeps a network that includes seventy of the most popular sites in the United States. Getting in is hard with the one-million-impression requirement, but lined with gold if you can do it. Close behind is 24/7 Media at **www.247media.com**. It also requires one million impressions per month. If that's not challenging enough, try qualifying for Adsmart at **www.adsmart.com** where the minimum to qualify is 2.5 million impressions per month. If you're getting more impressions than that, advertising bureaus will start contacting you. Do me a favor and mention this book when they call.

## Keeping Up with the Online Ad Industry

If you make money by advertising on your site, you should make sure you're current with the latest Internet advertising trends.

You can do that by bookmarking ad sites and browsing them periodically.

The Internet Advertising Bureau at **www.iab.net** is a not-for-profit association that seeks to increase the use and effectiveness of online advertising. Its site provides articles written by members who have studied various aspects of advertising and come up with tips for both advertisers and advertising sites.

If you want to see other ad networks and find out how one expert thinks they stack up against each other, visit **www.adbility.com**. Site host Mark Welch is a former attorney who became an e-commerce consultant in 1997 to help small Web publishers like you benefit from banner advertising. He has helped design affiliate advertising networks and knows all the hidden surprises that tricksters will try to put over on you. That's made him especially dedicated to helping you avoid getting burned. Spend some time clicking around Adbility and you'll discover which companies to avoid, which to pursue, and the best way to make advertising money based on the type of content your site provides.

Finally, don't forget that online advertising is still advertising, the same thing companies have been doing for ages. That being the case, take a peek at the ad industry's top rag, *Advertising Age* at **www.adage.com**. You'll find advertising news, helpful statistics on what's working, and possibly a few client leads. I read an article there recently that profiled companies looking to reach a demographic that my website happens to target. You might find a similarly useful list.

# 9 Happy Trails!

That about does it. You have all the information you need to start and maintain your own moneymaking website. If it becomes successful enough, you can hire a few people to make it even more successful.

Remember that the most important contribution you have to make to the Internet is your unique content. Properly packaged in a well-designed site with products that appeal to your visitors, that content will win the hearts of thousands. The sheer volume of Web traffic combined with the variety of human interest guarantees you an audience. Make a place for them, tell them about it, and welcome them when they arrive. Whatever prosperity comes your way will be well deserved.

**Your Site Will Win the Hearts of Thousands**

Perhaps as your first associate program product, you could sell this book through Amazon.com. Hey, that's a great idea! Whether you do that or not, I would like to hear about your success. Please e-mail me your Web address when your site is ready to go. I will list your address on my Web success page. My e-mail address is jkelly@jasonkelly.com.

For an updated list of resources and links to every address shown in this book, visit my site at **www.jasonkelly.com**. Happy trails to you, until we meet again.

Appendix

# Directory of Websites in This Book

For the online version of this directory with all sites linked for easy access, visit **www.jasonkelly.com**. I periodically add other resources that I didn't know about when writing this book.

## Advertising Agencies Specializing in the Internet (pp. 168–69)

- 24/7 Media
  **www.247media.com**
- Adsmart
  **www.adsmart.net**
- Ad-Up
  **www.ad-up.com**
- Burst Media
  **www.burstmedia.com**
- DoubleClick
  **www.doubleclick.net**
- Flycast
  **www.flycast.com**

## Advertising Campaign Management Services (p. 165)

- AdForce
  **www.adforce.com**
- Bondsmith
  **www.bondsmith.com**
- Central Ad
  **www.centralad.com**

## Advertising Information (p. 170)

- Adbility
  **www.adbility.com**
- Advertising Age Online
  **www.adage.com**
- Internet Advertising Bureau
  **www.iab.net**

## Affiliate Sales Programs (pp. 82–89)

- Amazon.com
  **www.amazon.com/associates**
- Anaconda
  **www.anaconda.net**
- Art.com
  **www.art.com/affiliates**
- Autoweb.com
  **www.autoweb.com/affiliate**
- Bach Systems
  **www.bachsys.com**
- Beyond.com
  **www.beyond.com/affiliates/index.htm**
- eToys
  **www.etoys.com/cgi-bin/affiliate form.cgi**

- Fogdog Sports
  **www.fogdog.com/affiliates**
- GiftTree
  **www.cj.com**
- iCreditReport.com
  **www.icreditreport.com/affiliate/affiliate.htm**
- JFAX
  **webtrans.jfax.com/affiliates**
- LendingTree
  **www.lendingtree.com**
- Magazines.com
  **www.magazines.com**
- MotherNature.com
  **www.mothernature.com/affiliate/default.asp**
- NextCard
  **banners.nextcard.com/affiliates/affiliates.shtml**
- One & Only
  **www.oneandonlynetwork.com**
- PulseTV
  **www.pulsetv.com/pan index.html**
- SendWine.com
  **www.sendwine.com/affiliate.asp**
- TravelNow.com
  **affiliate.travelnow.com/new/index.html**
- Web Cards
  **www.printing.com/bannerinstructns.htm**

## Affiliate Sales Program Directories (pp. 89–90)

- Associate It
  **www.associate-it.com**
- Associate Programs
  **www.associateprograms.com**

- ClickQuick
  **www.clickquick.com**
- SiteCash
  **www.sitecash.com**

## Affiliate Sales Program Networks (pp. 90–91)

- Be Free
  **www.befree.com**
- Commission Junction
  **www.cj.com**
- LinkShare
  **www.linkshare.com**

## Auction Sites to Sell Your Products Online (p. 116)

- Amazon.com Auctions
  **auctions.amazon.com**
- Auction Universe
  **www.auctionuniverse.com**
- eBay
  **www.ebay.com**
- Yahoo Auctions
  **auctions.yahoo.com**

## Autoresponse System (p. 117)

- AWeber
  **www.aweber.com**

## Banner Ad Exchange Networks (Free) (p. 149)

- Banner Co-op
  **www.bannerco-op.com**
- HyperBanner
  **www.hyperbanner.net**
- HyperExchange
  **www.hyperexchange.net**

- IntelliClicks
  **www.intelliclicks.com**
- LinkExchange
  **adnetwork.linkexchange.com**
- Massive Traffic
  **www.massivetraffic.com**
- RapidLinks
  **www.rapidlinks.com**

## Banner Ad Design Tools (p. 154)

- Animation.com
  **www.animation.com**
- Banner Tips
  **www.bannertips.com**
- Fireworks Software by Macromedia
  **www.macromedia.com/software/fireworks**
- QuickBanner
  **www.quickbanner.com**

## Browsers (p. 17)

- Internet Explorer
  **www.microsoft.com/ie**
- Navigator
  **www.netscape.com/download**

## Chat Rooms (p. 29)

- Chatcom
  **www.chatcom.com**
- Yahoo
  **chat.yahoo.com**

## Computer Stores (p. 11)

- Buy Computers
  **www.buycomp.com**

- Computers.com
  **www.computers.com**
- Dell
  **www.dell.com**
- Gateway
  **www.gateway.com**
- MicroWarehouse
  **www.microwarehouse.com**
- Onsale.com
  **www.onsale.com**
- Outpost.com
  **www.outpost.com**

## Content Syndication (pp. 72, 138)

- iSyndicate
  **www.isyndicate.com**
- Los Angeles Times New Media Division
  **www.timeslink.com**
- New York Times Syndicate
  **www.nytsyn.com/online**
- Ramius Network
  **www.ramius.net**

## Credit Card Acceptance (Merchant Account, p. 110)

- Cardservice International
  **www.cardservice.com**
- Data Transfer Associates
  **www.datatransfer.com**
- eCardNet
  **www.ecardnet.com**

## Domain Naming Services (pp. 41–43)

- Network Solutions
  **www.networksolutions.com**

- Unclaimed Domains
  **www.unclaimeddomains.com**

## E-mail Programs and Services (p. 18)

- Bigfoot
  **www.bigfoot.com**
- Eudora Light
  **www.eudora.com**
- Hotmail
  **www.hotmail.com**
- Juno
  **www.juno.com**
- USA.net
  **www.usa.net**
- Yahoo Mail
  **mail.yahoo.com**

## E-mail List Management (pp.134–35)

- ListBot
  **www.listbot.com**
- OneList
  **www.onelist.com**

## Hosting Services (p. 40)

- Digiweb
  **www.digiweb.com**
- Hiway Technologies
  **www.hiway.com**
- Hostpro
  **www.hostpro.com**
- WebHostList
  **www.webhostlist.com**

## Internet Service Providers (p. 16)

- AT&T WorldNet
  **www.att.net**
- Earthlink
  **www.earthlink.net**
- IBM Global Network
  **www.ibm.net**
- Mindspring
  **www.mindspring.net**
- WebISPList
  **www.webisplist.com**

## Marketing Sites (pp. 155–56)

- forkinthehead.com
  **www.forkinthehead.com**
- Hits to Sales
  **www.hitstosales.com**
- NETrageous
  **www.netrageousresults.com**
- PromotingYourSite.com
  **www.promotingyoursite.com**
- Promotion World
  **www.promotionworld.com**
- Sell It!
  **www.sellitontheweb.com**
- VirtualPROMOTE
  **www.virtualpromote.com**
- Web Marketing Information Center
  **www.webmarketingtoday.com/webmarket**
- WebPromote
  **www.webpromote.com**

## Message Boards (p. 29)

- Excite
  **boards.excite.com**
- Lycos
  **boards.lycos.com**
- Yahoo
  **messages.yahoo.com**

## Miscellaneous

- About.com on Honeymoons (p. 136)
  **honeymoons.about.com**
- About.com on Quilting (p. 27)
  **quilting.about.com**
- Allison's Cookies (p. 2)
  **www.allisonscookies.com**
- CarSmart (p. 169)
  **www.carsmart.com**
- Drudge Report (p. 53)
  **www.drudgereport.com**
- Frommers (p. 27)
  **www.frommers.com**
- Jason Kelly (p. 39, 63, 96–97)
  **www.jasonkelly.com**
- Legicrawler (p. 105)
  **www.legicrawler.com**
- Light Writer (p. 105)
  **www.lightwriter.com**
- Motley Fool (p. 27)
  **www.fool.com**
- Raging Bull (p. 27)
  **www.ragingbull.com**

- Salon (p. 125)
  **www.salon.com**
- ShopWeb.net (p. 100)
  **www.shopweb.net**
- SmartMoney (pp. 132–34)
  **www.smartmoney.com**
- Tellitagan (p. 104)
  **www.tellitagan.com**
- TheKnot (p. 137)
  **www.theknot.com**
- Tropi-Ties (p. 137)
  **www.tropi-ties.com**
- U.S. Census Bureau (p. 20)
  **www.census.gov**
- Yack (p. 169)
  **www.yack.com**

## Newsgroups (p. 32)

- CyberFiber
  **www.cyberfiber.com**
- Deja News
  **www.deja.com**
- Newsville
  **www.newsville.com**

## People Directories (p. 25)

- 555-1212
  **www.555-1212.com**
- AnyWho
  **www.anywho.com**
- BigBook
  **www.bigbook.com**

- ICQ.com
  **www.icq.com**
- InfoSpace
  **www.infospace.com**
- Sixdegrees.com
  **www.sixdegrees.com**
- SwitchBoard
  **www.switchboard.com**

## Press Release Distribution (p. 147)

- Businesswire
  **www.businesswire.com**
- PR Newswire
  **www.prnewswire.com**
- PR Web
  **www.prweb.com**

## Search Engines and Site Directories (pp. 19, 138)

- About.com
  **www.about.com**
- Alta Vista
  **www.altavista.com**
- America Online
  **www.aol.com**
- Excite
  **www.excite.com**
- HotBot
  **www.hotbot.com**
- InfoSeek
  **www.infoseek.com**
- Looksmart
  **www.looksmart.com**

- Lycos
  **www.lycos.com**
- Northern Light
  **www.northernlight.com**
- STPT
  **www.stpt.com**
- Yahoo
  **www.yahoo.com**

## Search Engine Rank Checkers (p. 127)

- Position Agent
  **www.positionagent.com**
- Rank This
  **www.rankthis.com**

## Search Engine Submission Services (pp. 121–23)

- Announce It
  **www.announceit.com**
- PostMaster
  **www.netcreations.com/postmaster**
- Search Engine Watch
  **www.searchenginewatch.com**
- SelfPromotion.com
  **www.selfpromotion.com**
- Submit It
  **www.submit-it.com**

## Stores to Sell Your Products Online (pp. 113–14)

- Yahoo Store
  **store.yahoo.com**
- iCat
  **www.icat.com**

## Website Tracking (p. 74)

- HitBox
  **www.hitbox.com**
- SiteTracker
  **www.sitetracker.com**
- StatMarket
  **www.statmarket.com**
- SuperStats
  **www.superstats.com**

## Website Tuning (pp. 69, 126)

- Key Word Count
  **www.keywordcount.com**
- NetMechanic
  **www.netmechanic.com**
- Web Site Garage
  **www.websitegarage.com**

## Website Features (pp. 67–68, 130, 135)

- BeSeen
  **www.beseen.com**
- Dynamic Drive
  **www.dynamicdrive.com**
- HotBot Tools
  **www.hotbot.com/help/tools**
- NetMind
  **www.netmind.com**
- Pollit
  **www.pollit.com**
- Recommend-It
  **www.recommend-it.com**
- SmartLinks
  **www.looksmart.com/smartlinks**

- Uproar
  **www.uproar.com/webdevelopers/intro.html**
- whatUseek
  **www.whatuseek.com/webmaster**
- Yahoo To Go
  **docs.yahoo.com/docs/yahootogo**

## Web Utilities (pp. 106, 121)

- MetaMedic
  **www.northernwebs.com**
- URL Manager
  **www.url-manager.com**
- Web Confidential
  **www.web-confidential.com**

## Web Graphics (p. 67)

- AAA Clipart
  **www.aaaclipart.com**
- Art Today
  **www.arttoday.com**
- Clipart.com
  **www.clipart.com**
- Really Big
  **www.reallybig.com/clipart.shtml**

## Website Design Contests (p. 147)

- Lycos Top 5%
  **point.lycos.com**
- Too Cool
  **www.toocool.com**
- USA Today Hot Sites
  **www.usatoday.com**

## Web Design Sites (pp. 57–58)

- About.com on Web Design
  **webdesign.about.com**
- BrainFind
  **www.brainfind.com**
- Builder.com
  **www.builder.com**
- Developer.com
  **www.developer.com**
- Dmitry's Design Lab
  **www.webreference.com/dlab**
- Efuse
  **www.efuse.com**
- Sitelaunch
  **www.sitelaunch.net**
- Webmonkey
  **www.hotwired.com/webmonkey**

## Web Design Software (pp. 47–48)

- Dreamweaver
  **www.macromedia.com/software/dreamweaver**
- Fusion
  **www.netobjects.com/products/html/nf4.html**
- GoLive
  **www.adobe.com/prodindex/golive/main.html**